COUNTRIES OF THE WORLD

Austria

Gareth Stevens Publishing
A WORLD ALMANAC EDUCATION GROUP COMPANY

About the Author: Marian Mazdra is an Austrian citizen who has worked in Vienna as a journalist and writer. She currently lives in Munich, Germany.

Written by
MARIAN MAZDRA

Edited by
LYNELLE SEOW

Edited in the U.S. by
CATHERINE GARDNER
ALAN WACHTEL

Designed by
JAILANI BASARI

Picture research by
THOMAS KHOO

First published in North America in 2005 by
Gareth Stevens Publishing
A World Almanac Education Group Company
330 West Olive Street, Suite 100
Milwaukee, Wisconsin 53212 USA

Please visit our web site at
www.garethstevens.com
For a free color catalog describing
Gareth Stevens Publishing's list of
high-quality books and multimedia programs,
call 1-800-542-2595 (USA) or 1-800-387-3178 (Canada).
Gareth Stevens Publishing's fax: (414) 332-3567.

© **MARSHALL CAVENDISH INTERNATIONAL (ASIA)**
PRIVATE LIMITED 2004
Originated and designed by
Times Editions Marshall Cavendish
An imprint of Marshall Cavendish International (Asia) Pte Ltd
A member of Times Publishing Limited
Times Centre, 1 New Industrial Road
Singapore 536196
http://www.timesone.com.sg/te

Library of Congress Cataloging-in-Publication Data
Mazdra, Marian.
Austria / by Marian Mazdra.
p. cm. — (Countries of the world)
Includes bibliographical references and index.
ISBN 0-8368-3115-2 (lib. bdg.)
1. Austria—Juvenile literature. 2. Austria—History—Juvenile literature. 3. Austria—Social life and customs—Juvenile literature.
I. Title. II. Countries of the world (Milwaukee, Wis.)
DB17.M39   2004
994—dc22   2004042878

Printed in Singapore

1 2 3 4 5 6 7 8 9 08 07 06 05 04

Contents

AN OVERVIEW OF AUSTRIA

A land of mountains and forests located at the center of Europe, Austria is renowned for its breathtaking beauty. The Austrian Alps dominate the landscape, overlooking the mountain hamlets and resorts that have become a haven for adventure seekers and ski enthusiasts during the winter months. This small country was once part of the vast and powerful Habsburg Empire and the seat of its Holy Roman emperors. Austria's fame today, however, is not in the rise and fall of its dynastic past but in its rich heritage in music, art, and architecture. Austrian culture is also evident in the country's stately opera houses, its country wine taverns, and its coffeehouses, in which coffee-drinking is both a favorite Austrian pastime and a high art.

Opposite: **Austrian children can learn to ski at any of the country's ski resorts during the winter.**

Below: **A couple takes a walk along a paved road located on Grossglockner, Austria's highest peak.**

THE FLAG OF AUSTRIA

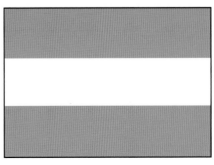

The Austrian flag consists of a central white band on a red background. According to legend, the colors of the flag were inspired by the bloodstained tunic of Duke Leopold V after the 1191 Battle of Ptolemais. It is said that the duke's white attire was stained red with enemy blood except for the area beneath his belt, inspiring the red-white-red colors of the Austrian flag. Austria actually has two national flags: the civil flag, which is used by the country's citizens, and the state flag, which is used by the Austrian government on official occasions. The state flag bears the traditional Austrian coat of arms — a black imperial eagle.

Geography

The Land

Austria is located at the heart of Europe. It is landlocked, sharing borders with eight countries: Germany and the Czech Republic, to the north; Switzerland and Liechtenstein, to the west; Slovenia and Italy, to the south; and Slovakia and Hungary, to the east. The country covers an area of 32,377 square miles (83,857 square kilometers) and is about twice as large as Switzerland.

Austria's terrain consists mainly of mountains and forests. The Eastern Alps dominate southern and western Austria. The northern and eastern parts of the country consist of hills and plains, particularly around the Danube Valley and Vienna, the Austrian capital city. Austria is one of the most heavily forested European countries, with woodland covering about half of the country.

The Eastern Alps

The Alps stretch across nine countries, from France and Italy, in their south, to Germany, Switzerland, and Austria, in their north. The section of the Alps known as the Eastern Alps covers about 63 percent of Austria and includes the Bavarian Alps along

THE ALPS

The Alps may span the territories of nine European countries, including Austria, but they form only a small part of a much larger, discontinuous mountain chain that extends from the Atlas Mountains in northern Africa to beyond the Himalayas in eastern Asia.

(A Closer Look, page 44)

Left: Mountains cover about two-thirds of Austria. The mountains of the northern and southern ranges of the Eastern Alps are short and rugged.

6

Left: **A lake in Tyrol is a source of freshwater fish. Lakes are popular during the summer as vacation spots.**

the Austria-Germany border and the Tauern Mountains in southern Austria. The Eastern Alps is home to Austria's highest mountain, Grossglockner, at 12,461 feet (3,798 meters).

The Alps form the backbone of Austria. Mountain passes, such as Brenner Pass, which connects Austria with Italy, enable travel through the Eastern Alps.

Rivers and Lakes

Austria's longest and most important river is the Danube (Donau) River, into which smaller rivers such as the Enns, Salzach, Drava (Drau), and Mur (Mura) Rivers drain. Although the Danube River's course through Austria is only 220 miles (350 kilometers) long, the river and its tributaries drain 96 percent of the country. The Danube River, the source of which is in western Germany, is the second longest river in Europe, running a course of 1,770 miles (2,850 km) across nine countries before reaching the Black Sea. The country's two largest lakes are Neusiedler Lake (Neusiedlersee), in the east, and Lake Constance (Bodensee), in the west. Neusiedler Lake is the country's lowest point.

THE DANUBE RIVER

In the past, the Danube River served as an important trade route between European countries. Today, it is harnessed for hydroelectric power. The river's majesty has been immortalized in a famous waltz, *The Blue Danube* (1867), by Austrian composer Johann Strauss the Younger (1825-1899).

NEUSIEDLER LAKE

Neusiedler Lake is shared by Austria and Hungary, although most of the lake lies in Austrian territory.
(A Closer Look, page 54)

Climate

Three different climatic systems affect different parts of Austria. The wet and temperate Atlantic climate influences western and northwestern Austria, particularly in the Danube Valley. Precipitation in these parts of the country is higher than it is in the eastern regions of Austria. Southern Austria is affected by a warmer Mediterranean climate. Eastern Austria, by contrast, is affected by the cold, dry Continental climate. As a result, this region receives the least amount of precipitation. Eastern Austria is also the least humid part of the country. Generally, humidity and precipitation levels are highest in western Austria and decrease as one moves eastward. Rainfall in the country is highest during summer, and short, heavy downpours are common.

Temperature and precipitation vary with altitude. In the lowlands and the hills of eastern Austria, the median temperature in January is 30.4° Fahrenheit (-0.9° Celsius). In regions above 10,000 feet (3,050 meters), the median temperature in January is 11.8° F (-11.3° C), and the precipitation is greater than at lower altitudes. Valleys, however, are often cold and foggy during the winter months, making the Alpine regions on a sunny day feel warmer and more comfortable. Occasionally, the Alpine snow melts suddenly because of a rapid change in temperature caused by warm, dry winds known as foehn.

FOEHN

A foehn is a warm, dry southern wind that moves rapidly northward across the Austrian Alps, causing temperatures to increase suddenly. When foehns blow during the winter, the snow cover melts quickly, triggering avalanches. It is believed that foehn can affect people's moods and cause headaches.

Plants and Animals

Forty-seven percent of Austria is covered in forests. Oak and spruce trees dominate the lower altitudes, while beech and fir trees are found at altitudes above 1,600 feet (488 m). Fir, larch, and stone pine trees can be found at altitudes above 4,000 feet (1220 m). Alpine and foothill regions are usually forested with coniferous trees, while the warmer regions support leafy deciduous trees. Flowers such as the edelweiss can be found in Alpine meadows located above 6,560 feet (2,000 m).

The country's animal life is rich and varied. Red deer, marten, and gamebirds are common forest animals. Brown bears, eagles, falcons, and storks are protected by conservation laws. Chamois, ibex, and marmots are common Alpine animals. Neusiedler Lake, located in eastern Austria, is a haven for bird species, such as the purple heron and the avocet. The country's many rivers support rainbow trout, perch, and carp.

National Parks

Austria has six national parks, which cover 3 percent of the country. The largest national park is the Hohe Tauern National Park, with an area of 690 square miles (1,787 square km). Almost one-quarter of Austria consists of nature reserves and park land.

Left: The edelweiss flower is found in Alpine regions. The flower has six to nine lance-shaped white leaves arranged in a star. It is believed that young suitors used to climb onto the rocky crags of the Alps to pick edelweiss flowers for girls they liked.

History

Human settlement in the Danube area dates back centuries, but little is known about the earliest settlers in the region. In 400 B.C., Celtic tribes invaded the land, forming the first state in the region, known as Noricum, in what is today central and southern Austria. The Romans were attracted to Noricum, which was well-known for its lucrative salt and ore trades, and occupied the region in 15 B.C.

Roman control over the region gradually weakened as migrations of different tribes, such as the Huns and the Germans, crossed the land. In the fifth century, the Romans withdrew from the region after five hundred years of occupation. The following years saw further tribal migrations and settlements, as well as the Christianizing of the Alpine regions. In the eighth century, Charlemagne, king of the Franks, gained control of the land.

Above: **Frederick III was the Holy Roman Emperor and the fifth duke of Austria.**

The Babenbergs

The Babenbergs, a Bavarian dynasty, began to rule Austria in 976 A.D. They reached the height of their power in the twelfth century and formed a large part of the Austrian nobility. The death of Frederick II, who left no heir or male successor, in 1246

THE HABSBURG LIP

Members of the Habsburg family had a physical trait that became prominent with Emperor Frederick III. The emperor had a protruding jaw and lower lip, causing his mouth to open slightly. This trait, known as the Habsburg Lip, became more and more pronounced in successive generations because the Habsburgs inbred in order to preserve a pure Habsburg lineage.

Left: **In 774 A.D., Charlemagne (*left*) was crowned in a ceremony held in Pavia, Italy.**

Above: **Charles I (*right*) was the last of the Habsburg rulers. He reigned for three years before going into exile with his wife and family in 1919.**

marked the end of Babenberg power. The Bohemian king, Otakar II of the Premysl dynasty, married one of the last of the Babenberg women and ruled Austria until his death in 1278. In 1282, the Holy Roman emperor, Rudolf von Habsburg, granted his two sons the rule of Austria, thereby laying the foundation for Habsburg control in the country for the next six hundred years.

The Habsburgs

The Habsburgs were a German royal family who moved their family seat from Switzerland to Austria. The family became known as the House of Austria because it gained extensive land in and around the country through marriages that extended its influence. The lands under the Habsburg Empire became known as the Hereditary Lands, and they included most of Austria and parts of Germany, Italy, France, Croatia, and Slovenia. In 1452, Frederick III was elected emperor of the Holy Roman Empire. Over the following three hundred years, every Holy Roman emperor was a Habsburg. The succession of Holy Roman emperors from the Habsburg line strengthened the reputation of the House of Austria throughout Europe.

Habsburg Gains and Losses

The marriage of Frederick III's great-grandsons, Ferdinand and Karl, to heiresses resulted in the further expansion of the Habsburg empire into Austro-German and Spanish-Dutch lines. The Habsburg Empire reached the height of its power in the sixteenth century. Roman Catholicism played an important part in unifying the Hereditary Lands.

In 1700, the Spanish Habsburg line ended with the death of Charles II of Spain. Charles VI, the last male Habsburg of this period, died in 1740 and was succeeded by his daughter, Maria Theresa. During the eighteenth and nineteenth centuries, Austria went through a series of upheavals caused by the French Revolution, the Napoleonic Wars, the disintegration of the Holy Roman Empire, and the emergence of the nation of Italy. All of these changes led to the gradual loss of Habsburg power.

In 1867, the Habsburg Empire was divided into two parts: the Austrian lands and Hungary. These two regions were collectively known as Austria-Hungary or the Austro-Hungarian Empire. In 1914, following the assassination of the Habsburg heir to the throne, Franz Ferdinand, and his wife in Sarejevo by Bosnian nationalists, Austria-Hungary declared war on Serbia. Other European countries were drawn into the fray, and the conflict escalated into World War I.

THE PRATER

Once used as a hunting ground exclusively for Austrian royalty, the massive area known as the *Prater* (praht-EHR), located just outside the heart of the city of Vienna, is now a public park used by a wide variety of local people.
(A Closer Look, page 56)

Left: Archduke Franz Ferdinand and his wife were in Sarajevo on June 28, 1914, when they were assassinated. During World War I, Austria-Hungary, Germany, and Turkey formed the Central Powers, which fought for four years against the Allies.

Left: Nazi soldiers humiliated Jews by forcing them to scrub the pavement in Vienna. By the end of World War II, about 81,000 Austrian citizens, including 65,000 Austrian Jews, had been murdered in Nazi concentration camps.

Democratic Austria, Nazi Austria

In 1918, the Allies defeated Austria-Hungary and the other Central Powers. The Treaty of Saint-Germain was signed in 1919. This treaty ended the Habsburg Empire and established the new boundaries of the newly-named Republic of Austria. As a result of the treaty, Austria, Hungary, Czechoslovakia, Poland, and Yugoslavia became independent countries. In 1920, provincial representatives and leaders drew up Austria's Federal Constitution. In 1925, the Austrian schilling became the country's new currency.

The new republic faced political problems between its two major parties, the Christian Social Party and the Social Democratic Workers' Party. In 1938, Nazi Germany seized Austria. Adolf Hitler proclaimed the *Anschluss* (AHN-SHLOOS), or union, of Austria to Germany. Austria's fate was thus tied to Nazi Germany, whose quest for power led to World War II. Under Nazi control, Austrian Jews and political leaders were sent to concentration camps, while others had their possessions confiscated. About 130,000 Austrians fled the country, and more than 247,000 Austrian soldiers died serving in the German army.

THE TRAPP FAMILY

The Sound of Music, a popular musical and Hollywood film has become a well-loved classic. The story was inspired by the experiences of a real family that left Nazi-occupied Austria.

(A Closer Look, page 68)

A Neutral Center

After the Allies defeated Germany in 1945, Austria became a republic again. Under the supervision of the Allies, Austria formed a democratic government that included leaders from the Austrian People's Party (the former Christian Social Party), the Socialist Party of Austria (the former Social Democratic Workers' Party), and the Communist Party of Austria. This coalition stabilized the country's government. In 1955, Austria signed the State Treaty, which ended the Allied occupation in the country and restored Austria's sovereignty. Under the treaty, Austria would not be allowed to unify with Germany or restore the Habsburg rulers. In the same year, Austria declared itself a neutral country and became a member of the United Nations (UN).

As a neutral country, Austria has served as a mediator between the non-Communist countries of Western Europe and the Communist countries of Eastern Europe. Since 1960, the country has also been involved in at least thirty peace support operations. Austria has served twice on the UN Security Council and has been elected to the governing boards of various UN agencies. In 1995, Austria became a member of the European Union (EU). The country held the presidency of the EU Council in 1998.

Left: **The UN Building in Vienna is an important international conference center. In 1979, one of three UN headquarters was built in Vienna. The other two are in New York City and Geneva, Switzerland.**

Bertha von Suttner (1843–1914)

Bertha von Suttner was a writer and peace activist. Her novel *Die Waffen nieder* (Lay Down Your Arms), published in 1889, influenced the public greatly with its portrayal of the horrors of war. In 1873, Bertha became the governess of the young daughters of the von Suttner family. She fell in love with the family's youngest son, Baron Arthur Gundaccar von Suttner, who was seven years her junior, and they were engaged to be married. In 1876, she went to Paris to work as a secretary to Alfred Nobel, but returned to Vienna a week later to marry the baron. She continued, however, to correspond with Nobel on the progress of the peace movement and to participate in peace conferences. It is believed that her great influence on Nobel led him to establish the Nobel Peace Prize, which she was awarded in 1905 for her active involvement in the peace movement.

Bertha von Suttner

Ignaz Seipel (1876–1932)

Ignaz Seipel was Austria's chancellor from 1922 to 1924 and from 1926 to 1929. A Roman Catholic priest by training, Seipel was the most important Austrian politician between the years after World War I and the Anschluss because of his role in Austria's postwar economic recovery. In 1922, Seipel secured a loan of U.S. $100,000,000 from the League of Nations, an international body established by the Allies. The loan stabilized the Austrian currency and curbed inflation in the country. Seipel, however, supported fascist currents in Austrian politics. In 1924, Seipel was wounded during an assassination attempt.

Ignaz Seipel

Bruno Kreisky (1911–1990)

Bruno Kreisky joined the Social Democratic Party of Austria in 1926. He was imprisoned several times for his political activities in the 1930s. In 1970, he became the Austrian chancellor. As the leader of the Social Democratic Party of Austria (SPÖ) — known until 1991 as the Socialist Party — Kreisky successfully put the country's declaration of "permanent neutrality" into effect. Under his leadership, Austria improved its world standing by playing a larger role in mediating international affairs. Kreisky retired in 1983, after thirteen years of leadership.

Bruno Kreisky

Government and the Economy

Austria is a federal republic made up of nine self-governing states, or *Länder* (LEN-der): Burgenland, Carinthia, Lower Austria, Salzburg, Styria, Tyrol, Upper Austria, Vorarlberg, and the country's capital, Vienna. The head of state is the federal president, who is elected by popular vote to serve a six-year term. The president appoints the federal chancellor, who is the head of the government, and the cabinet members. The cabinet appoints judges to the country's three high courts. Austrian courts are independent of the country's parliament and its head of state.

The Austrian parliament consists of the National Council (Nationalrat) and the Federal Council (Bundesrat). The National Council is the main legislative body and consists of 183 members who are elected by the country's citizens to serve four-year terms. The Federal Council consists of 62 members who are chosen according to the size of their respective states. Federal Council members represent the interests of their states.

VIENNA

Vienna is Austria's political and cultural capital. The city is located at the northeastern tip of Austria. Most of the city lies on the eastern bank of the Danube River.
(*A Closer Look, page 70*)

Below: Vienna is the country's capital and the seat of the Austrian government. Because it is both a city and a state, its mayor also serves as its governor.

Left: **The Austrian parliament consists of the National Council and the Federal Council. National Council members are voted into the parliament by the country's citizens. All Austrian citizens age nineteen or older may vote.**

Political Parties

The four political parties represented in the National Council are the Austrian People's Party (ÖVP), the Social Democratic Party of Austria (SPÖ), the Freedom Party of Austria (FPÖ), and the Green Alternative (GA). The ÖVP received 42.3 percent of the votes in the National Council's 2002 election, winning 79 out of the 183 seats.

State Governments

Each state has its own state government, which is headed by a governor and also includes deputies who help to run the state's administration. State legislation, however, is run by a body known as the *Landtag* (LAHND-tahg), or land parliament. State laws passed by the Landtag must be certified by the state governor. The federal government must also give consent to Landtag legislation if the proposed state laws involve it.

The Austrian Federal Constitution

Austria's Federal Constitution was drawn up in 1920 and states that Austria is a democratic republic that derives its authority from its people. The country's constitution is based on the principles of democracy and the separation of judicial and legislative powers. It also guarantees civil rights and freedoms, such as freedom of the press and freedom of worship.

WELFARE SYSTEM

The Austrian government runs a comprehensive social security and welfare system. Health and other insurance programs are available to nearly the entire population. Those people not covered by the insurance system can receive welfare benefits.

Left: Tourism is a key industry in Austria. Many shops sell local hand-crafted products. Austria first adopted the euro as its currency in 1999. In 2002, the Austrian schilling was completely replaced by euro bills and coins.

Economy

Austria has a free market economy. The country is one of the wealthiest in the EU, and its standard of living is high. Austria has a developed industrial sector, natural resources, and a low unemployment rate.

The state owns one-quarter of Austria's economy, including heavy industries, such as steel manufacturing, and public services companies, such as Austria's telecommunications company, Telekom Austria. Since 1997, however, some state-owned businesses have been privatized. The remaining three-quarters of the economy consists of medium-sized businesses that specialize in manufacturing, trade, and light industries, such as food processing. The industrial sector provides 33 percent of the country's gross domestic product (GDP) and employs 29 percent of Austria's labor force of 4.3 million people. In workshops throughout Austria, skilled craftsmen produce glassware, jewelry, and other handicrafts to supply active tourist and export markets.

Service businesses make up the country's largest economic sector. They account for 65 percent of the Austria's GDP and employ 67 percent of its workforce. The service industry makes up a large portion of the GDP because of tourism and the increase in foreign investment after Austria joined the EU in 1995. Foreign investments stimulated the Austrian banking and financial sectors to provide business services, leading to economic growth.

TRADING PARTNERS

Austria does most of its trading with the surrounding EU countries: Germany, Italy, and France. Its other trading partners include Switzerland, the United States, and Hungary. Germany is Austria's main trading partner. Major Austrian exports include machinery, automobiles, metal goods, paper, lumber, textiles, iron, steel, and chemicals. The country imports oil and electricity. Although Austria produces its own food, it imports foreign foodstuffs as well.

Natural Resources

Austria is the world's biggest producer of natural magnesite, a white mineral used by its chemical industry. The country is also rich in lead, zinc, and iron. Iron ore is mined in Styria and processed in industrial centers throughout the country. Steel and iron are important export products, and they are also used by Austrian industries, including its vehicle and industrial machinery industries. Austria is known for its iron and steel construction industries, and the Austrian steelmaking process is used by steelworks around the world.

Almost half of the country is covered in forests, making timber a vast and easily available resource. Paper mills and timber processing plants are found throughout Austria, and the processed timber is exported.

Austria meets part of its energy needs with its own deposits of coal, petroleum, and natural gas, but additional fuel must be brought into the country through pipelines. Austria's hydroelectric power plants produce 67 percent of the country's electricity, making Austria the largest producer of hydroelectric power in the EU.

Farms occupy less than 20 percent of the country. Only 41 percent of the country's land can be cultivated, because Austria's terrain is mountainous. Although agriculture provides only 2 percent of the country's GDP, its agricultural sector supplies 80 percent of Austria's domestic food requirements.

SALZKAMMERGUT'S "WHITE GOLD"

"White gold" brought prosperity to the Austrian region in which this precious commodity was mined. It was so valuable that visitors were banned from entering the mining region until the nineteenth century in order to prevent anyone from smuggling any "white gold" out.

(A Closer Look, page 60)

Left: Fresh produce grown in Austria can be found in local markets around the country. Austria produces grains, wine, fruit, and potatoes, as well as cattle and poultry. Four percent of the country's labor force works in its agriculture and forestry sectors.

People and Lifestyle

Austria has a population of about 8.2 million people. Ethnic Germans form the great majority, making up 88 percent of the total population. Due to its high percentage of Germans, Austria is considered a homogenous society. Austrians, however, differ in physical appearance. Some are fair-skinned, blond, and blue-eyed, while others are dark-skinned with brown eyes.

Croats, Hungarians, Czechs, Slovaks, Slovenes, and Roma are minority ethnic groups in Austria. They live mostly in eastern and southern Austria, but many have also migrated to Vienna, which is home to large communities of Czechs, Slovaks, and Turks. Austria's Slovenes usually live in Carinthia, and the country's Croats usually live in Burgenland. In the second half of the twentieth century, many eastern Europeans sought refuge in Austria either because they were expelled from their countries or because they wanted to escape economic hardship. In 1989, the country experienced an influx of eastern European refugees.

LIFE EXPECTANCY

In 1970, the Austrian life expectancy was 60 years for males and 73 years for females. Today, it is about 76 years for males and over 81 years for females. Life expectancy has increased, while birth rates have fallen. It is estimated that by 2035, one-third of Austrians will be over 60 years old.

Below: A winter carnival event in the city of Telfs involves pouring food and drink over men as part of the fun.

Gemuetlichkeit

Above: **In Austria, it is common to see families and friends sharing a meal together outdoors.**

Gemuetlichkeit (GEH-moot-lihk-EYET) is the very relaxed enjoyment of life that is the typical Austrian attitude. It is common to see Austrians sitting at a sidewalk café sipping coffee and watching people as they walk past. These activities are examples of Gemuetlichkeit, which involves enjoying the day slowly, either alone or in the company of family and friends.

Austrian Abodes

Most Austrians live in eastern Austria, in the lower areas of the country where temperatures are warmer. About one-fifth of the population lives in Vienna. The country's second-largest city after Vienna is Graz, the capital of the state of Styria. City dwellers in Austria often live in apartment buildings or in single-family homes. In rural areas, people live mainly in single-family houses. Houses in Austria differ in style and architecture according to the region in which they are built.

About ten percent of Austrians own vacation homes, which are usually located outside the city. An Austrian vacation home may be a traditional rural house or a small single-story house surrounded by a small garden. They are used for recreation or relaxation on weekends and holidays.

FARM HOLIDAYS

Some families who want to spend a weekend or vacation in the Austrian countryside choose to vacation on a farm. Different types of farms cater to various recreational interests.
(A Closer Look, page 50)

Family

Austrian families are usually small. Most Austrian parents have only one or two children, often due to the high cost of living in the cities. Larger families are more common in rural areas. Since the 1970s, families have become smaller, and divorce rates have increased. In 2002, the divorce rate was 44.4 percent. This means that almost half of all Austrian marriages ended in divorce. The number of single-parent families in the country also has increased since the 1960s. In 2001, 13 percent of Austrian families were single-parent families.

Austrian Women

According to Austrian law, women have the same rights as men, and there are no legal constraints on women. It is not unusual, however, for Austrian women to earn less than their male counterparts, even when they do the same work. Women are also less likely to hold high-level jobs.

Traditional families, in which the wife manages the household while the husband goes to work, are still fairly common in Austria. Educated women, however, are moving away from their traditional roles as housewives to establish careers outside the home. As a result, women are marrying later and having children at a later age. The Austrian government provides extensive support for women choosing to have children. For example, women are entitled to sixteen weeks of paid maternity leave and receive free medical care during pregnancy and after childbirth.

The rise in the number of single-parent families has forced the Austrian government to provide financial aid for these families. Unwed mothers receive more government benefits than married mothers. Many Austrians believe that the policy goes against their culture's traditional family values because it encourages people to have children outside of marriage.

Marriage

Austrians are marrying later. In 1980, the average marrying age for men was about twenty-six, and for women, about twenty-three. In 1991, the average marrying age rose to twenty-eight for men and twenty-six for women, and in 2001, the average marrying age was thirty for men and twenty-seven for women.

Above: **Single-parent families are increasingly common in Austria today.**

BABY NAMES

In 2002, the most popular Austrian male baby name was Lukas, followed by Florian and Tobias. Lukas has been a popular baby name since 1996. For girls, Anna was the most popular name, followed by Sarah and Julia, which was the most popular name for baby girls from 1988 to 2001.

Opposite: **A mother and her two children feed swans by a lake on a lazy afternoon.**

Education

In 1774, Maria Theresa issued an edict to increase literacy among the people. Under her plan, education was no longer just a privilege of the upper class. It was made available to all, regardless of social class. Since 1962, all children in the country must attend school between the ages of six and fifteen. In 2004, Austria had a literacy rate of 98 percent.

Austrian children begin their nine-year compulsory education in *Volksschule* (FOLK-schoo-luh), or elementary schools, which are either private or state-run. State-run schools provide education free of charge. Children start schooling at age six. They attend the Volksschule for four years and begin to study a foreign language, such as French or English, in the third year. At age eleven, students can choose to move on to secondary level education at either a four-year *Hauptschule* (HOWPT-schoo-luh), or middle school, or an eight-year academic secondary school, which prepares students to attend a university. Secondary academic schools provide a general education, and students in these schools study subjects such as mathematics, music, art,

Left: Physical education is a required subject from the first through the twelfth years of school in Austria. Students can take ski courses and swimming lessons. Both public and private schools teach physical education. Private schools in Austria are usually parochial. About 10 percent of all schools in Austria are private.

science, foreign languages, and computer science. At the end of their final year, graduates are awarded the *Reifeprüfung* (REYE-feh-PROO-foong), which is the diploma they need to enter Austrian universities after passing their final exams.

Secondary level graduates from both Hauptschule and secondary academic schools can continue their education at technical and vocational schools around the country. Some join apprenticeship programs to learn specialized skills to prepare them for working life. In addition to these programs, the country has fifty teachers' training colleges, twelve music conservatories, two military academies, and other specialized colleges. Austria also has nineteen universities, including universities specializing in art and music. The accessibility of universities has resulted in many Austrians pursuing higher education. Women account for half of the Austrian university-student population.

The Austrian government today is refining the education system, both to give schools more autonomy and to meet the demands of today's world. The Austrian school curriculum now incorporates media education and the use of computers.

Above: **The University of Vienna, founded in 1365 by Rudolf IV, is the country's oldest and largest university. It is also one of the oldest universities in central Europe. Nine Nobel laureates have had academic careers at the University of Vienna. Austrian universities have produced numerous Nobel prize winners, such as Fritz Pregl, who won the Nobel Prize in Chemistry in 1923.**

Religion

Christianity was introduced to Austria in the second century, largely due to the expansion of the Roman Empire. In the sixteenth century, the religious conflict between Catholics and Protestants during the Protestant Reformation ended in victory for the Catholic Habsburgs. The Habsburgs suppressed the Protestant faith and forced their religion on everyone under their control. Since then, Austria has been a mainly Roman Catholic country. Even today, the majority of Austrians — about 78 percent — are Roman Catholic, and only about 5 percent are Protestant. Muslims make up 4.2 percent of the population, partly because of the influx of Turkish immigrants in the 1990s. Since 1867, all Austrians have enjoyed freedom of religion.

Austrian Roman Catholics

After the eighteenth century, Austria recognized twelve other religious communities, including Jews, Muslims, and practitioners of Orthodox faiths. Despite the presence of these religious communities in the country, Austria and the Vatican maintained close ties. The Roman Catholic Church

Below: **In a town near Salzburg, Roman Catholics celebrate Corpus Christi with a procession outdoors.**

Left: **A memorial at the Mauthausen Concentration Camp in Upper Austria commemorates the Austrian Jews who perished at the hands of the Nazi regime.**

wielded considerable influence in the country, especially before 1918. Today, the influence of the Roman Catholic Church in Austria has waned. Church attendance is low, and the teachings of the Roman Catholic Church on issues such as abortion and divorce go unheeded by many Catholics. Most Austrian Roman Catholics, however, continue to celebrate traditional Christian religious holidays, such as Christmas and Easter.

Austrian Jews

At least 7,000 Jews live in Austria today, most of whom reside in Vienna. In 1938, however, the Jewish population of Austria numbered about 200,000, and represented 4 percent of the country's population. After the union with Nazi Germany in the same year, about 100,000 Jews fled the country before the start of World War II. Among them was Sigmund Freud, a leading figure in Austria's cultural and intellectual life. Beginning in 1941, the Jews that remained in Austria were arrested and sent to Eastern European ghettos or deported to Nazi concentration camps, such as Dachau and Buchenwald, where they were killed. About 65,000 Austrian Jews perished in the Holocaust. After World War II, some surviving members of Austria's Jewish population returned to the country.

PSYCHOANALYSIS: THE THEORY OF SIGMUND FREUD

The theories of Sigmund Freud, the father of psychoanalysis, became the foundation for treating mental disorders for many years. Freud fled Austria when the Nazi's invaded the country in 1938.

(A Closer Look, page 58)

Language and Literature

German is Austria's official language, and almost all Austrians speak German as a mother tongue. The German spoken in Austria is slightly different from the German spoken in central Germany. Within the country, Austrians from different regions speak their own local dialects, which are derived from Austro-Bavarian, a language closely resembling German. The dialect of one Austrian region can sound very different from a dialect spoken in another Austrian region. This means that an Austrian from Vienna speaking *Wienerische* (VEE-ner-RISH-eh) may have trouble understanding an Austrian from Vorarlberg speaking *Vorarlbergerische* (for-ARL-BER-ger-ish-eh).

In order to communicate effectively between regions, Austrians use a standardized form of German, called *Hochdeutsch* (hoch-DOYTCH), or High German. Hochdeutsch refers to the German spoken in the mountainous (*hoch*) regions of Germany, Austria, and Switzerland. Hochdeutsch is sometimes referred to as standard German. Regional variations of Hochdeutsch, however, also exist within Austria.

Left: Two women dressed in traditional finery during a regional festival stop to chat. Austrian dialects that vary from province to province are commonly used, although German is the official language of Austria. Minority languages spoken in Austria include Croatian and Hungarian. Each of these languages has its own dialects as well.

Austrian Literature

The Habsburg Empire and the Roman Catholic Church influenced the development of Austrian literature, not only in the early twelfth and thirteenth centuries, which were marked with a flourishing of sacred and royal poetry, but in the centuries to come. During the reign of Maria Theresa in the eighteenth century, the arts flourished in Austria. Vienna, in particular, became an intellectual and cultural center.

In the late nineteenth century, Austrian literature began to express a greater Austrian identity with the establishment of the *Sezession* (ZEH-zee-on) movement. Austrian life at the turn of the century was portrayed by writers such as Hugo von Hofmannsthal, whose play, *Jedermann*, is the highlight of the annual Salzburg Festival.

The collapse of the powerful Austro-Hungarian empire in 1918 marked another turning point for Austrian art and literature. Writers, such as Karl Kraus and Joseph Roth, captured the uncertainty felt by Austrians during this period.

Since 1945, Austrian literature has been varied. Controversial Austrian writer Thomas Bernhard explored themes of death, social injustice, and human suffering in postwar Austria. Austria's internationally recognized contemporary authors include Ingeborg Bachmann, Ilse Aichinger, and Peter Handke.

Arts

Austria is known throughout the world for its contributions in architecture, fine arts, and music. The arts received generous patronage by generations of Habsburgs, and the country continues to support the arts today.

Architecture

The Roman Catholic Church had a strong influence on Austria's architecture. Cathedrals became showcases for the most talented architects and the latest architectural styles. Early cathedrals, such as the twelfth-century St. Stephen's Cathedral, located in Vienna, were built in the Romanesque style. St. Stephen's Cathedral was later reconstructed in the gothic style, which is characterized by towering, pointed arches. In the sixteenth century, architecture took a turn for the dramatic and theatrical with the baroque style. Baroque architecture was heavily ornamented, and it inspired a new era of Austrian architecture. Austrian architect, Johann Bernhard Fischer von Erlach combined different architectural styles, including the baroque style, to form a new style called Austrian baroque. The baroque style later developed into the even-more-ornate rococo style.

BAROQUE ARCHITECTURE

Austria is a showcase of baroque architecture. The city of Vienna has some of the best examples of this style in the world.
(A Closer Look, page 47)

ART NOUVEAU

Art nouveau is an ornamental style that was popular between 1890 and 1910. In Austria, the movement was called Sezessionstil, while in Germany, it was called Jugendstil. The style made use of motifs derived from nature. Flower stalks, vines, and tendrils are common in art-nouveau decoration.

Left: St. Stephen's Cathedral in Vienna is a cultural and architectural landmark. Its colorful roof stands in eye-catching contrast to its pointed gothic arches.

Left: A street artist creates a chalk portrait of a woman on the sidewalk in the city of Innsbruck.

Below: A contemporary apartment building in Vienna combines art with architecture.

Otto Wagner was a leading figure of the Austrian art-nouveau movement. During the late nineteenth and early twentieth centuries, Adolf Loos developed a simplified style of architecture marked by clean lines, flat surfaces, and no ornamentation. His work strongly influenced the European modern movement. Contemporary Austrian architects include Hans Hollein and Coop Himmelblau, both of whom have won international recognition.

Painting

Movements in Austrian architecture and art were closely related in the nineteenth and twentieth centuries. In 1897, a group of artists led by painter Gustav Klimt broke away from academic art and formed a group known as the Vienna Sezession. The Sezessionists set the stage for modern Austrian artists such as Egon Schiele and Oskar Kokoschka to emerge. Klimt developed a new style known as Austrian expressionism, which culminated in the works of Schiele and Kokoschka. Austrian expressionism aims to capture the artist's emotional state in a painting. Austrian artists in the second half of the twentieth century included painters Siegfried Anzinger and Max Weiler.

GUSTAV KLIMT

Gustav Klimt is not only one of Austria's most celebrated painters but also the founding father of the Vienna Sezession, an important movement in Austrian art.

(*A Closer Look*, page 52)

Music

Austria is the birthplace of one of the greatest composers in the history of classical music — Wolfgang Amadeus Mozart. Considered a musical genius, Mozart composed various types of music, making him one of the most versatile composers in the history of Western classical music. Mozart's friend and fellow Austrian, Joseph Haydn, is credited as the father of the symphony and string quartet. Haydn founded the Viennese classical school and tutored the famous German musician, Ludwig van Beethoven.

The waltz, a dance that developed from Austrian country dance, became popular in Viennese ballrooms in the eighteenth century. Johann Strauss the Elder made the waltz the ballroom dance of the European bourgeoisie, but it was his son, Johann Strauss the Younger, who was known as "the Waltz King."

In the nineteenth century, Austrian composers such as Franz Schubert, Anton Bruckner, and Gustav Mahler, helped initiate a new musical era. The leading pioneer of classical music in that era, however, was Austrian-born American Arnold Schoenberg.

CLASSICAL MUSIC

Austria has a legacy of music. Many classical-music heavyweights are associated with Vienna, which for many centuries has been the classical-music capital of the world.
(*A Closer Look*, page 48)

AUSTRIA'S NATIONAL ANTHEM

Joseph Haydn composed the song *God Save the Emperor Franz*, which was performed on the emperor's birthday, in 1797. It was Austria's national anthem until 1918. In the late 1920s, new words were written for the melody, and it again became the country's anthem. In 1947, Austrians chose a new national anthem, the melody of which was drawn from the work of Wolfgang Amadeus Mozart.

Left: A boy plays the violin on a street in Vienna. Austrian musicians have a rich past to draw from.

Austria today continues to make important musical contributions. The country's Vienna State Opera and the Vienna Philharmonic Orchestra continue to be among the best in the world and contribute to Austria's enduring image as a land of music. The highly-acclaimed Vienna Boys' Choir, which has existed since 1498, holds concerts and sings every Sunday at Mass in Vienna's Hofburg chapel.

The 1970s saw the rise of contemporary Austrian singers, such as Johann Hölzl, who became famous under the name of Falco. Singers like Wolfgang Ambros and Georg Danzer created a style of music called Austropop in the German-speaking world.

Above: **The Vienna Opera House is the venue for many performances by the world-renowned Vienna Philharmonic Orchestra.**

Theater

Many Austrian musicians also wrote for the theater. Mozart wrote sixteen operas, one of which was *Don Giovanni*. Johann Strauss the Younger was famed for his operettas, which became popular in Vienna in 1870. Operettas are light, amusing operas with spoken dialogue. Viennese operettas reached their height with the work of composer Franz Lehár. The close relationship between music and drama in these works can be seen at the Salzburg Festival, Austria's most prestigious arts festival.

Leisure and Festivals

Sports are part of the Austrian lifestyle. The country's 27,000 sports clubs cater to different sporting preferences. The country's beautiful landscapes are the scene of many summer and winter recreational activities. The most popular of these include hiking, swimming, skiing, cycling, tennis, soccer, horseback riding, and golf. These activities help Austrians relax and stay healthy. The Austrian government funds sports facilities and subsidizes sports clubs, which are used by about three million people throughout the country. Tennis courts and swimming pools are found in both large cities and small towns.

Enjoying Austria's Great Outdoors

Hiking and mountaineering are popular pastimes in Austria during the warm months. Well-marked hiking trails crisscross the country, running through various terrains. Alpine trails are dotted with mountain huts for hikers who follow routes that may take several days to complete. The country's ten mountaineering clubs have about 450,000 members. Cycling along Alpine roads is also popular. The Tour d'Autriche is an annual cycling race that covers 930 miles (1,500 km) through Austria's mountains.

THE SPANISH RIDING SCHOOL

Founded in the sixteenth century, the prestigious Spanish Riding School in Vienna is the world's oldest equestrian school. The school is known to the locals as Spanische Hofreitschule.

(A Closer Look, page 64)

Left: Sunbathing at a lake is a popular summer activity. In addition to Austria's many lakes, the country also has six national parks, numerous nature reserves, and many hiking resorts to satisfy the Austrian love for hiking and the outdoors.

Left: Austrian tennis player Thomas Muster returns a ball to his opponent in the Mallorca Open tennis tournament held in Spain in 1998.

Competitive Sports

Austrians perform well in many competitive sports. Many of the country's people are athletes. Austrian athletes have won numerous medals in international competitions such as the Olympics. Since 1924, Austria has won 41 gold medals in the Winter Olympics. In the 2000 Summer Olympics, held in Sydney, Australia, Austria won two gold medals in sailing. Peter Seisenbacher represents the best of Austrian judo, having been an Olympic medalist in 1984 and 1988. In 1996, Austrian tennis player Thomas Muster briefly ranked first in the world in tennis. Muster's success began in 1984, when he became the Austrian national champion at the age of seventeen. His rise in the international tennis rankings was achieved by winning numerous tennis tournaments, including the 1995 French Open. He retired from professional tennis in 1999. In motor racing, Niki Lauda was the Formula One champion in 1975, 1977, and 1984. Austrians, however, seem to do particularly well in winter sports, such as skiing, which is one of Austria's most popular recreational activities.

SOCCER

Soccer is widely played in Austria, but the country's successes in international soccer have been few and far between. In 1954, the Austrian national team placed third in the World Cup competition. One Austrian soccer player, Ernst Happel (1925–1972), gained international repute as a coach for various Dutch and German professional teams. In 2008, Austria and Switzerland will host the UEFA European Championship.

Winter Fun

During the winter months, Austria's mountain ski resorts are populated by avid skiers and snow boarders. Ice skating, tobogganing, sledding, and bobsled racing are also popular. Sitting by a fire and soaking in a hot spa at any of Austria's famous Alpine resorts are popular relaxing winter activities.

The country is credited as the birthplace of modern downhill skiing. In 1897, an Austrian, Matthias Zdarsky, wrote the world's first ski-instruction manual. Since then, Austria has been at the forefront of skiing techniques and instruction. Since World War II, skiing in the mountains has become more accessible because of the development of ski lifts and cable cars. Today, these lift facilities are available even in glacier regions, enabling passionate skiers to ski even in the summer.

Austrian professional skiers and ski jumpers are well-known for their outstanding performances. Austrian skiers, such as Toni Sailer, Karl Schranz, and Franz Klammer, have won medals in the Olympics and other world championships.

Austria's reputation as one of the leading skiing nations has earned the country the opportunity to host various European and world competitions. In 1964 and in 1976, Innsbruck was the site

SKIING IN AUSTRIA

Skiing is an Austrian tradition and passion. Austria is also a magnet for winter sports enthusiasts from around the world and a popular destination for European youths attracted by its well-known ski slopes.
(A Closer Look, page 62)

Left: Children can ice skate in the square in front of Vienna's City Hall. The square becomes a rink during the winter, after it is filled with water.

Left: **The Viennese coffeehouse is an age-old institution. Anyone can spend the whole day in a Viennese coffeehouse reading, conversing, or people-watching.**

of the Winter Olympics. In 1991, the Alpine Skiing World Championships were held in the state of Salzburg, and in 1996, the Ice Hockey World Championship was held in Vienna. More recently in 2001, St. Anton am Arlberg hosted the Alpine Skiing World Championships.

Social Haunts

Social life in Austria is characterized by Gemuetlichkeit. Summer days can be spent in city parks or in the forests of the countryside. In the evenings, beer gardens and *Heurigen* (HOY-rih-GEHN), or wine taverns, are popular gathering places.

The most famous of Austrian social haunts, however, is the Viennese *Kaffeehaus* (KAH-fay-HOWSS), or coffeehouse. To Austrians, the coffeehouse is more than a place for sampling different types of coffee. It is an extension of their living rooms. It is a place to relax, read newspapers, play chess, meet friends, write poems, and people-watch. Coffeehouses are where Gemuetlichkeit is most evident, and they are important places in Austrian life and culture.

WINE TAVERNS

Called Heurigen, Austrian wine taverns are run by local winemakers who take pride in their products, selling only what they make themselves. Each tavern has a character that is as distinctive as the wines served there. Heurigen serve as social places for Austrians to get together and share an evening of food and wine.

(A Closer Look, page 72)

Festivals

Because most Austrians are Roman Catholic, church-related festivals and holidays are celebrated in the country throughout the year. During Lent, Easter markets sell decorated eggs and braided pussy-willow branches called *Palmkätzchen* (palm-KETZ-chen). On Palm Sunday, the Sunday before Easter, Catholic Austrians attend Mass and get their Palmkätzchen blessed by the priests. The Palmkätzchen are said to be symbols of rebirth.

Christmas festivities begin with Advent, the period leading up to Christmas. Advent is a festive time, during which homes are decorated with wreaths made of twigs. In late November, city squares and streets become Christmas markets, which sell all types of Christmas fare from cotton candy to roasted chestnuts.

Traditionally, on Christmas Eve, the adults in a family decorate the Christmas tree, which the children are not allowed to see. Once a family has finished their Christmas dinner, a bell is rung to announce the arrival of the Christ-child, who brings the Christmas gifts. Girls may receive a gown, which they will wear if they attend a ball. At midnight, Catholic families attend a Mass, during which they sing "Silent Night." Austrians spend Christmas day with family and friends, who are invited over to share a traditional meal of roast goose.

SILENT NIGHT

The popular Christmas carol "Silent Night," was composed in 1818 by Franz Xaver Gruber, an Austrian schoolmaster. Gruber composed the tune on his guitar on Christmas Eve in St. Nikolai's Church, located in Oberndorf, a village near Salzburg. Today, "Silent Night" has been translated into 320 languages and is sung all over the world.

FASCHING

Fasching (fah-SHING) is the period between Epiphany and Ash Wednesday. In some regions, it begins as early as November 11. In Tyrol, some people believe that wearing masks during Fasching will chase away the evil spirits of winter. Elsewhere in Austria, Fasching is celebrated with elaborate carnivals, in which there is music, dancing, and fancy dress parades. The end of Fasching is marked by setting piles of wood on fire.

Left: Men wear masks and costumes at a Fasching carnival parade in Tyrol.

Left: A couple waltzes during a waltz festival. Festivals and holidays play a major role in Austrian life.

Austrian festivals are not only about celebrating religious holidays but also about celebrating Austria's rich cultural life. Fasching, or Carnival, is the season for balls. The year starts with the Kaiserball at Vienna's Imperial Palace. Between January and February, many Austrians spend their evenings waltzing at balls, decked out in formal wear or in traditional *Trachten* (TRAHK-tun). The highlight of the season is the lavish Opera Ball in February, which is held at the Vienna Opera House.

Arts Festivals

Austria has at least nine music festivals throughout the year. Concerts of all types of music, including operas and operettas, attract local and international audiences, especially during the summer months. Music festivals include the Bregenz Festival, at Lake Constance, and the Danube Festival, in Krems, which features regional music, dance, and theater.

The country's most prestigious and renowned arts festival is the Salzburg Festival, held in Salzburg. World-class operas, plays, and concerts are performed over a period of five to six weeks each summer. The festival has attracted thousands of people since 1920, when it was first held.

TRACHTEN

Trachten are the national dress of Austria and were inspired by the clothing of the nation's country folk. Austria's urban dwellers began to wear Trachten in the late nineteenth century.
(*A Closer Look, page 66*)

Food

Austrian food is heavily influenced by German, Czech, Italian, and Hungarian cuisine. Meat and dumplings are the usual fare, although freshwater fish, such as trout and walleye from the country's lakes and rivers, are also popular. Each state has its own culinary speciality. Upper Austria is famous for *Knödel* (NOH-dehl), or dumplings, which are filled with savory or sweet ingredients, such as cheese or apricots. Dumplings are also enjoyed in soups. It is, however, Viennese cuisine — particularly, its pastries and cakes — that has earned Austria its good culinary reputation,

The Wiener schnitzel, which is usually a veal cutlet that is breaded and then fried until golden-brown, is a traditional Austrian meat dish. *Tafelspitz* (TAH-fehl-SPEETZ), or boiled beef, is another Austrian favorite. The local *Gulasch* (GOO-lahsh), a beef stew served with bread and dumplings, is a less spicy Austrian adaptation of the heavily-spiced Hungarian goulash. *Wiener Backhendel* (VEE-nah BAHK-hayn-dl), or Viennese fried chicken, is a Viennese specialty that is commonly served at Heurigen.

Left: **The Wiener schnitzel is a fried breaded veal cutlet. Pork and turkey are sometimes used instead of veal.**

Austrian adults usually enjoy their meals with a mug of beer or a glass of wine. The Wachau Valley, located between the towns of Melk and Krems in the Danube Valley region, is one of the country's primary grape-growing regions. In areas closer to Germany, such as Innsbruck and Salzburg, beer is preferred over wine. Breweries, which also serve light meals, serve as social places for Austrians to get together.

Above: **Viennese tortes and pastries are world famous. Tortes are rich cakes made from a mixture of finely chopped nuts and eggs that use little or no flour.**

Sweet Treats

One of the most well-known Austrian desserts is the *Apfelstrudel* (ahp-FEHL-stroo-DEHL), or apple strudel, which is a baked pastry filled with apples and raisins. The *Sachertorte* (SAH-kehr-TOHR-teh) is a rich chocolate cake. Its original recipe, created by Franz Sacher, is kept secret by the Hotel Sacher, which is located in Vienna. An assortment of tortes and strudels are often served with coffee during the afternoon in Vienna's coffeehouses.

Christmas pastries include *Vanillekipferl* (van-ill-leh-KIP-fuhrl), or vanilla crescents, and Christmas fruit bread. These, as well as other homemade treats, are sold at Christmas markets throughout the country during the Christmas season.

A CLOSER LOOK AT AUSTRIA

Austria is a land of natural and human-made beauty. The Austrian Alps provide a dramatic backdrop for the country's cities and towns. Lakes, meadows, and forests dot the country, and farmhouses and wine taverns nestle in the picture-perfect Austrian countryside. The jewel of Austria, however, is its capital — Vienna. The city is home to some of the greatest examples of baroque architecture in the world. Gothic spires decorate the city's skyline. Vienna is also a city of music and dance. During the annual ball season, Viennese ballrooms glitter with waltzing couples. In the past, Austria was a leader in music and art

Opposite: **A musical procession in the Austrian countryside features band members dressed in traditional clothes.**

movements. Austrian musicians, architects, and artists, such as Wolfgang Amadeus Mozart, Johann Bernhard Fischer von Erlach, and Gustav Klimt, have defined new eras in their respective fields.

    The Austrian landscape is both beautiful and majestic, as well as exciting and fun. From riding a slow ferris wheel at the Prater to skiing down Alpine slopes at breakneck speeds, the country offers many activities. Austria's mountains, lakes, cities, and people are as much a part of Austria's culture as the sound of its music.

Above: **Austrians look on as a game of chess played on a giant chess board in the city of Salzburg progresses.**

The Alps

The Alps are a complex mountain system that spreads over nine countries — Austria, Bosnia and Herzegovina, Croatia, France, Italy, Germany, Switzerland, Slovenia, and Yugoslavia. The Alps, which measure about 750 miles (1,207 km) in length and cover an area of more than 80,000 square miles (207,200 square km), are divided into three sections: the Western, Central, and Eastern Alps. Austria's peaks are part of the Eastern Alps.

Two-Thirds of Austria

In Austria, the Alps dominate the country's landscape, occupying nearly two-thirds of the country's area. The Austrian Alps can themselves be further divided into northern, central, and southern sections. The Bavarian Alps form part of the northern section, while the Carnic and Julian Alps form part of the southern section.

Mountains in the central section are mostly composed of granite and are generally taller than those in the northern and southern sections. At higher altitudes, the central mountains are covered with crystal-like rocks that make the edges appear less jagged. The Hohe Tauern Mountains and the Ötztal Alps form part of the central Austrian Alps. Standing at 12,375 feet (3,772 m), Wildspitze, the tallest of the Ötztal Alps, is also Austria's second-

Left: At the Hohe Tauern National Park, well-marked hiking trails take hikers across rivers and through beautiful forests.

Left: **Austria is home to 270 of the 600 ski resorts that operate in the Alps today. In an attempt to reduce the harm done to the land by traditional tourists every ski season, Austrian authorities today are encouraging ecotourism in the Alps.**

highest peak. The country's highest and third-highest peaks, Grossglockner and Grossvenediger, respectively, are both part of the Hohe Tauern Mountains. Grossvenediger measures 12,054 feet (3,674 m) high and is about 400 feet (122 m) lower than Grossglockner. Grossglockner is also famous for being home to a spectacular glacier called the Pasterze (PAHST-ehrtss).

Human Activity and Irreparable Damage

The history of human settlement in the Alps dates back to Paleolithic times, which were some 50,000 to 60,000 years ago. Over time, the early inhabitants of the Alps developed a lifestyle and economy that was centered on agriculture, which included the cultivation of fruits and vegetables and the raising of cattle. Nineteenth-century industrial developments, including the production of hydroelectricity, led parts of the Alps, including western Austria, to focus on mining and manufacturing instead of agriculture. Beginning in the mid-1900s, commercial tourism grew to become a major source of income for many people who lived in the Alps. Relentless human exploitation over the last two centuries, however, has caused irreparable damage to the Alps' natural environment. Air, water, and noise pollution, as well as slope erosion, have reached unprecedented levels. At the start of the twenty-first century, the Alps were identified as the world's most threatened mountain system.

Baroque Architecture

Austria is home to beautiful examples of baroque architecture built hundreds of years ago. The baroque style is an architectural style that was popular from the early seventeenth century to the mid-eighteenth century. It is a highly decorative style characterized by heavy ornamentation and vivid colors. Baroque architecture is dramatic and energetic compared to the classical architectural style. In Austria, the baroque style was adapted to suit Austrian taste in buildings, resulting in a distinctive style known as Austrian baroque.

Austrian Baroque

Austrian baroque architecture began with Austrian architect and sculptor Johann Bernhard Fischer von Erlach. Educated in Rome, Fischer combined forms from the classical, Renaissance, and Italian and French baroque styles, to create a restrained and monumental style that suited Habsburg taste. He designed magnificent, stately buildings that represented Habsburg power and control. Soon, he was sought by the Austrian aristocracy and the Roman Catholic Church to build palaces and churches. Under commission by the archbishop of Salzburg, Fischer helped shape the skyline of the city of Salzburg with his beautiful churches, especially the Kollegienkirche (University Church), which was completed in 1707. In Vienna, his works include the Winter Palace of Prince Eugene of Savoy.

Late Baroque Architecture

Johann Lucas von Hildebrandt (1668–1745) and Jacob Prandtauer (1660–1727), both of whom were well-known during the baroque and late-baroque periods, followed Fischer. The late baroque, or rococo, architectural style was a progression from the baroque and was even more decorative. It appealed to the aristocratic taste. Pastel colors were favored over vivid ones, and interiors were more graceful and refined. Sculpture and painting were important in rococo architecture, and frescoes and painted stucco surfaces were typical in rococo buildings. Hildebrandt introduced new decorative motifs and became famous for his decorations on building exteriors.

Above: **One characteristic of late baroque architecture is the painted façade. Pastel colors, such as yellow and pink, are common, along with ornamental scrolls, vines, and leaves.**

JOHANN BERNHARD FISCHER VON ERLACH (1656–1723)

Johann Bernhard Fischer von Erlach was born in Graz, Austria, in 1656 to a sculptor father. In his teens, he went to Rome and studied under the great baroque architect Gian Lorenzo Bernini, who shaped his early thinking. In 1687, Fischer began a career as court architect for three successive Holy Roman emperors: Leopold I, Joseph I, and Charles VI.

Opposite: **The Karlskirche (Church of St. Charles Borromeo) in Vienna was designed by Fischer. Gilded ornamentation, oval windows, and curved lines are used in baroque architecture.**

Classical Music

Austria is a world center of classical music. For centuries, music filled the city of Vienna and the royal courts of the Habsburgs. The country has produced world-famous musicians and composers whose works are as enduring today as they were in the eighteenth century. German composers such as Ludwig van Beethoven (1770–1827), Johannes Brahms (1833–1897), and Richard Strauss (1864–1949) were no less associated with Vienna than the Austrian composers Joseph Haydn (1732–1809), Franz Schubert (1797–1828), Johann Strauss the Elder (1804–1849), and Johann Strauss the Younger. These composers fill the pages of western classical music history. The most famous Austrian composer is Wolfgang Amadeus Mozart (1756–1791).

The Classical Age

The classical age of music began in the second half of the eighteenth century with the compositions of Haydn and Mozart. The music of this age was dignified, clear, and more restrained than the grand tunes of the preceding era. Haydn and Mozart, together with Beethoven, form what is known as the Viennese classical school or the first Viennese school.

WOLFGANG AMADEUS MOZART

Mozart was born in Salzburg in 1756. His father was a composer. Young Wolfgang began to show signs of his musical talent at the age of three. Two years later, he began composing tunes. When he was six years old, he performed in Vienna for the imperial court and the aristocracy. Mozart lead a short but creative life. When he died in 1791, he left behind an impressive number of musical works, including 16 operas, 32 concerti, 19 masses, 25 string quartets, and 41 symphonies.

Left: Mozart began playing the harpsichord when he was three years old. He is regarded as a musical genius.

The Romantic Age

The romantic age of music began in the nineteenth century. The compositions of this era were characterized by a greater freedom in composition and form. Music began to express more emotion, and inspiration was often drawn from nature. Haydn's life spanned the classical age and the start of the romantic age, but it was Franz Schubert who dominated the bridge between the two ages. Schubert, who is often called a romantic classicist, was a genius in composing melodies. He wrote more than six hundred songs in his short lifetime. His most famous symphony is his *Symphony in B Minor*.

The second half of the nineteenth century is called the late-romantic age. Compositions were more dramatic and used more harmonic variations. This age was influenced by the second Viennese school of music, founded by Austrian-born Arnold Schoenberg (1874–1951). Together with his pupils, Alban Berg and Anton von Webern, Schoenberg trimmed the excesses from the romantic school of the nineteenth century and led classical music into the twentieth century.

Above: **A monument to the Austrian composer Johann Strauss the Younger stands in Stadtpark in Vienna.**

THE BLUE DANUBE

The Blue Danube (1867) is a waltz composed by Johann Strauss the Younger (1825–1899). The waltz became popular as a ballroom dance in the nineteenth century. Waltz music and the dance itself are characterized by movement in 3/4 time. Strauss, his father, and his brothers dominated European ballrooms for centuries with their compositions.

Farm Holidays

Instead of renting a room in a hotel, many visitors to Austria spend their vacations on farms. Austria has thousands of farmhouses that cater to tourists and locals wishing to experience farm life. Many of Austria's farms are located in the country's beautiful countryside. There, vacationers can hike or swim in the summer or ski during the winter.

Different farms cater to different groups of people. Some farms are more suited for families. These farms may have farm animals that children can pet or play with. Children can learn how to milk a cow or feed sheep at these farms. Some farms are located by lakes or beaches. Families vacationing at these farms in the summer enjoy swimming in the lakes or catching fish.

Horse farm holidays are popular with children. Austria has about 150 farms that specialize in horse farm holidays. At these farms, children learn how to ride a horse and groom it. In the winter, they also take sleigh rides. In the warmer months, they go on riding trips in the countryside or in the mountains.

Below: **More than 3,000 farms in Austria are open to visitors.**

Austrian adults may prefer wine farms, which are located in the states of Styria, Burgenland, and Lower Austria. While vacationing at a farm, they may spend their evenings at a local Heuriger, sampling the regional food and the newest wine of the year. Many hosts also serve their guests their own estate wine.

Local Hospitality

The wide variety of farms often surprises people. Farm experiences range from active to relaxing. A farm holiday can also be a more affordable alternative to hotels and resorts. The common thread in all farm vacations is the opportunity to interact with the hosts and learn about the way they live. Some hosts offer insights into traditional farm crafts or skills, while others share the customs and culture of their region and trade. Each farm provides its guests with an adventure that includes activities ranging from milking cows and picking grapes to hiking or horseback riding.

One of the most memorable of farm-vacation experiences is enjoying a home-cooked meal made with the freshest ingredients. Some farms serve organic foods, which are grown without chemicals. Environmentally-friendly farms may have their own gardens, where the owners grow their own vegetables. Health farms may offer hay wraps and other spa treatments.

Gustav Klimt

A Rising Star

Born in Baumgarten, a region near Vienna, to a poor family on July 14, 1862, Gustav Klimt became one of Austria's most celebrated painters. Both Gustav and his brother Ernst were trained at the Vienna School of Decorative Arts. In 1883, the two brothers set up Künstlercompagnie, which means the "Company of Artists," with their contemporary, Franz von Matsch. The company specialized in mural paintings and was paid by a number of patrons to decorate the interiors of certain churches, theaters, and museums. Examples of Gustav Klimt's early works include murals at the Kunsthistorisches Museum and the Vienna Burgtheater, the latter of which he completed in 1888.

The Vienna Sezession and After

In 1897, Gustav Klimt and architects Josef Hoffman and Joseph Olbrich started the Vienna Sezession, a movement that encouraged artists to abandon the norms in academic art at the time. Similar to art nouveau, works reflecting the ideas

Left: Klimt poses for the camera with his cat. On February 6, 1918, Klimt died at age fifty-five after failing to recover from a stroke he suffered on January 11 of the same year.

Left: The Kiss (1908) celebrates intimacy between a man and woman. Themes in Klimt's paintings include love, sexuality, regeneration, and death. His paintings were sometimes controversial. In one particular incident, Klimt was asked to paint the ceiling of an auditorium of the University of Vienna. Klimt's contribution, which consisted of three paintings, titled *Philosophy*, *Medicine*, and *Law*, drew sharp criticism after they were unveiled. Klimt's three paintings, which were viewed as having pessimistic and erotic qualities, were rejected. As a result, Klimt never accepted another public commission in his life.

of the Vienna Sezession are typically highly decorated, with intricate patterns that come together to form curving lines. Klimt is believed to have started the movement because he felt that he had not been true to himself as an artist. In the eight years after the birth of the Vienna Sezession, Klimt produced several notable paintings, including the *Beethoven Frieze* (1902) and the murals in the Stoclet House, a lavish private mansion in Brussels.

In 1905, Klimt and a handful of other artists withdrew from the Vienna Sezession and formed another group called Kunstschau, which means "art show." Kunstschau nurtured some of Austria's most applauded twentieth-century painters, including Egon Schiele, Oskar Kokoschka, and Alfred Kubin. Klimt painted some of his most acclaimed pieces — including *Frau Fritza Riedler* (1906) and *Frau Adele Bloch-Bauer* (1907), both of which are portraits of rich and fashionable Viennese women of the time, and *The Kiss* (1908) — after forming Kunstschau.

IN GALLERIES THROUGHOUT THE WORLD

Today, Klimt's works are admired around the world. Many of his pieces are on display in galleries or museums in the United States, Canada, Italy, Israel, the United Kingdom, and Japan. In Austria, Klimt's key works are showcased at the Belvedere Palace, which is located in Vienna.

Neusiedler Lake

Neusiedler Lake is about 22 miles (35 km) long and between 4 and 9 miles (6 and 14 km) wide. Covering an area of about 135 square miles (350 square km), the lake is very shallow, with depths that generally do not exceed 6 feet (1.8 m).

Austria's Lowest Point

Known to the locals as Neusiedlersee, Neusiedler Lake straddles eastern Austria and northwestern Hungary. In Austria, the lake is in the state of Burgenland and is the site of the country's lowest point, which is 377 feet (115 m) above sea level. The Hungarians call the lake Ferto-tó, which means "swamp lake." In 1873, construction began to connect the lake to the Rabnitz River, which is a tributary of the Danube River, by way of a canal. The project took twenty-two years to complete. The Neusiedler Lake is believed to be supported by underground sources in addition to a modest supply provided by a small stream. The lake's water is slightly salty and does not have a natural drainage outlet.

Above: **A stork nests on the chimney of one of the Neusiedler Lake region's resorts.**

Left: **Ecotourists and birdwatchers come to Neusiedler Lake to see wildlife. The Neusiedler Lake region has resorts that cater to ecotourism.**

National Park Neusiedlersee (Seewinkle)

Reeds, or tall grasses with straight stalks, are plentiful along the lake's shores. This vegetation provides a natural environment that attracts many species of birds, helping the area to earn the reputation as a "bird paradise." The birds — many of them rare and some migratory — are protected by local laws and international regulations. Austrian authorities have sought to protect the lake and the wetlands around it beginning as early as the 1930s. In 1977, the United Nations Educational, Scientific, and Cultural Organization (UNESCO) declared the lake and its surrounding area a biosphere reserve. Six years later, the World Conservation Union (IUCN) declared the UNESCO reserve Austria's first internationally recognized national park. In November 1992, after negotiations with Austrian and Hungarian land owners, the local government of Burgenland passed the National Park Act. National Park Neusiedlersee (Seewinkel) covers an area of about 15 square miles (40 square km).

Above: **Reeds along the shores of Neusiedler Lake supply cellulose to Austrian industries. The reeds also attract migratory birds.**

The Prater

From Royal Hunting Ground to Public Park

The Prater occupies an area of some 3,200 acres (1,295 hectares) near the center of the city of Vienna. It was originally a hunting and riding ground for Austrian royalty. In 1766, Emperor Joseph II opened the Prater to ordinary Austrians. Today, the massive public park remains unfenced and includes a fairground packed with attractions that please both young and old; a stadium and swimming pool, for exercise enthusiasts; and diverse natural landscapes, such as woodlands, green meadows, and the Danube's riverbank, for those who prefer to unwind at a slower pace. Since becoming the Volksprater (VOHLKS-praht-EHR), or the People's Prater, in the mid-eighteenth century, the former royal playground has become a center for the leisure activities of Viennese Austrians.

Left: **The Riesenrad is a huge ferris wheel located in the Prater. A ride in one of the Riesenrad's fifteen cabins gives a stunning view of the city.**

Fairground Attractions

The giant ferris wheel known as the Riesenrad is probably the most prominent landmark inside the Prater. Built in 1897, the Riesenrad has fifteen cabins, each of which reaches a height of about 200 feet (61 m) above the ground. The Riesenrad, which turns at a speed of about 26 inches (65 centimeters) per second, was designed by British engineer Walter Basset, who was inspired by France's Eiffel Tower, which was built ten years earlier.

Winding through parts of the Prater is the Liliputbahn (lee-lee-PUT-BAHN), or Lilliputian railroad, on which miniature steam trains operate to carry people to relatively nearby locations. Each train takes about twenty minutes to travel the entire length of the railroad tracks, which measures about 2.6 miles (4.1 km).

An amusement park, a bicycle rental service, a miniature golf course, and some outdoor cafés also operate in the fairground. Not far from the Riesenrad is the building of the Prater Planetarium, inside of which is also the Prater Museum. While the museum is the place to learn about the Prater's history, the Planetarium offers a visual spectacle using state-of-the-art technology. The Planetarium's new projector is one of eight of its kind in the world and has the ability to bring images of parts of the galaxy onto the planetarium screen with great clarity.

Above: The amusement park behind the Riesenrad has a mix of old and new rides, from nostalgic merry-go-rounds and haunted castles to ultramodern thrill rides, such as the Tornado and Superman.

Psychoanalysis: the Theory of Sigmund Freud

Sigmund Freud is credited as the founder of psychoanalysis. Psychoanalysis is both a theory of how the human mind works and a treatment for people with mental disorders. Freud believed that people developed mental disorders, called neuroses, because they cannot resolve the conflict between what he considered to be the three aspects of human personality: the id, the ego, and the superego. The id is a person's basic instinct to pursue the satisfaction of one's desires, while the superego is made up of values, ideals, and behavior considered acceptable to a person's culture and society. The id and the superego are always in conflict. The ego must manage the two such that the id is sufficiently satisfied without disrupting the superego. A person develops a neurosis, according to Freud, when the ego fails to manage the id and the superego. Freud theorized that many types of neuroses occur when people repress their desires because these desires are considered socially unacceptable. These repressed

SIGMUND FREUD (1856–1939)

Sigmund Freud was born in what is today the Czech Republic. In 1860, his family moved to Vienna, where Freud spent the next 78 years of his life. In 1881, he graduated with a degree in medicine from the University of Vienna. He began his career as a physician, specializing in diseases of the nervous system. During his lifetime, he developed his theory of psychoanalysis and wrote numerous books about his findings and theories. In 1900, he published *The Interpretation of Dreams*, which many psychologists regard as his most important book. When the Nazis invaded Austria in 1938, they banned his theories and burned his books because he was a Jew. He escaped to London, England. In 1939, Freud died of cancer of the jaw and palate in London.

Left: Sigmund Freud looks through a manuscript in his home in Vienna.

Left: **Alfred Adler (1870–1937) was closely associated with Sigmund Freud, but broke away from Freud in 1911. Adler theorized that some individuals suffer from feelings of inferiority, and that these feelings can lead to neuroses.**

desires emerge as symptoms known as neurotic symptoms. Neurotic symptoms can range from depression to physical symptoms such as headaches and paralysis.

Freud used his theories to create a way of treating neuroses. One of his key ideas was that repressed desires are expressed in dreams. Freud taught his patients to use a method called free association to talk about their dreams. In free association, patients are instructed to say whatever comes to their minds about their dreams. The information gathered through free association is then used to figure out what the dreams symbolize. Understanding the symbols in dreams, Freud thought, would allow patients to understand the origins of their neurotic symptoms and change their behavior.

Followers of Freud's theories became known as "psychoanalysts." Other prominent psychoanalysts included Freud's daughter, Anna, and the Austrians Alfred Adler and Otto Rank. For decades psychoanalysis was considered one of the best treatments for neuroses. Because psychoanalysis takes a great deal of time and is very expensive — and because many modern psychologists doubt Freud's theories — psychoanalysis is not as popular as it used to be. Freud, however, is still considered a pioneer and an important thinker in the history of psychology.

Salzkammergut's "White Gold"

The Austrian region of Salzkammergut (sahltz-KAH-MAIR-goot) in northern-central Austria has been famous for its "white gold" for at least 4,500 years. Austria's white gold is also known by a more ordinary name — salt. Salt, though common today, was rare and precious centuries ago. The people of Salzkammergut mined and sold the sought-after commodity, and the region became prosperous. The region derived its name from the salt deposits found in the settlements of Hallstatt, Bad Ischl, and Bad Aussee. "Salzkammergut" means "salt chamber's possessions."

The Development of Hallstatt

The town of Hallstatt derived its name from the Celtic word for salt — *hal*. Salt mines were first established in 1200 B.C. Initially, the early miners transported the lumps of salt in fur bags. Later, the mined salt was transported via the Traun River, a

Below: **The town of Hallstatt is located on a lake. The region is well known for it beauty and its archaeological significance. In 1997, UNESCO made the Hallstatt-Dachstein-Salzkammergut region a World Heritage Site.**

tributary of the Danube River, to processing centers downriver. In 1595, the workers at Hallstatt built a pipeline out of thousands of hollowed wooden logs to transport the mined salt 25 miles (40 km) away to the town of Ebensee for processing. This pipeline is the oldest pipeline in the world.

Archaeological evidence indicates that salt mining was the main economic activity at Hallstatt for centuries. Today, Hallstatt is a beautiful, affluent town. The town owes its prosperity to its centuries-old, lucrative salt trade.

"The Man in Salt"

In 1846, a mine manager named Johann Geor Ramsauer uncovered an ancient cemetery at Hallstatt. Over the next 53 years, more than two thousand graves containing evidence of the early miners were found. Archaeologists also uncovered an ancient salt mine, which contained clothing and other objects the salt preserved. In 1734, a fully preserved body of a miner was found in the Hallstatt salt mine. The miner, unofficially called "The Man in Salt," is believed to have died at around 300 B.C.

AUSTRIA'S LAKE DISTRICT

The Salzkammergut region comprises parts of the states of Upper Austria, Styria, and Salzburg. The region is often referred to as the country's "Lake District" because it is home to more than thirty lakes, including Hallstätter Lake, along which is found the small town of Hallstatt.

Skiing in Austria

Austria is one of the best places in the world to go skiing. Each year, crowds of tourists and locals take to the slopes to engage in this exhilarating sport. World-class ski resorts dot the Austrian Alps, and during the winter months, cities and towns teem with professional and amateur skiers.

Serious work on making the mountains accessible to skiers began after 1945. At that time, the country only had a few mountain railways and six ski lifts. By 1998, the number of ski lifts had increased to 3,300. Villages and towns adapted to the crowds of tourists by building ski facilities and resorts. Today, the country is an internationally-acclaimed winter wonderland.

Ski Towns

One of the most popular Austrian towns for winter sports is Innsbruck, a city located at the foot of the Alps. Innsbruck is considered the global winter-sports capital, and the city lives up to its reputation. Winter sports of all kinds can be enjoyed at

Below: **Skiers prepare for an afternoon of fun on the Tyrolean slopes. Another popular ski destination is 38 miles (60 km) from the city of Salzburg. The Salzburger Sportwelt is at the center of Austria's largest linked ski area. The area consists of 540 miles (870 km) of ski runs and includes 270 modern ski lifts.**

Innsbruck, from snowboarding to cross-country skiing. Ice games such as curling — a game in which two teams of four players each use brooms to try to slide a stone to a target at the end of the rink — are also popular. The Arlberg region, located near the Rhaetian Alps, is a winter playground for members of European high society.

The Arlberg Technique

Historically, Alpine skiing began in the Arlberg region with the teachings of Austrian ski instructor Hannes Schneider. His technique, which became known as the Arlberg technique, influenced generations of skiers and ski instructors. Schneider invented a technique that enabled Alpine skiers to better handle Austria's Alpine terrain. As a youth he noticed that the Nordic ski technique, which uses an erect posture and rigid knees, did not work well in the Alps. Schneider's skiing technique, known as the Arlberg technique, combines a crouched posture in which the skier leans forward with many turning movements. Using the Arlberg technique, skiers can descend the Alpine terrain with great speed.

Above: Alpine resorts rent out skis to the hundreds of tourists and locals who come to enjoy a vacation in the mountains.

HANNES SCHNEIDER

Hannes Schneider (1890–1955) was born in Stuben am Arlberg. He founded a ski school in St. Anton am Arlberg, at which he taught his ski technique. The Nazis seized his school during the Anschluss. In 1938, Schneider fled to the United States and started a ski school in New Hampshire. He trained ski instructors and helped popularize skiing in the United States.

The Spanish Riding School

The World's Oldest Equestrian School

Founded in 1572, the Spanish Riding School is located in Vienna. Throughout its history, the school has sought to set the highest standards in the arts of training horses and horseback riding. At the beginning of the twenty-first century, the Spanish Riding School was the only institution in the world that still taught dressage in its most traditional form. Dressage is the style of horseback riding in which the rider guides the horse through precise movements with very subtle signals. At the Spanish Riding School, it has remained unchanged for four centuries.

The Spanish Riding School was so named because the early ancestors of the impressive white stallions that are still ridden at the school today originated in Spain. The prized white horses later became known as *Lipizzaner* (lee-pee-ZAH-nehr) horses after the stud farm in Lipizza (in present-day Slovenia) where they were bred for Austrian royalty. Today, Austria has a stud farm in Piber that specializes in caring for Lipizzaner horses.

Left: Riders perform a dressage at the Spanish Riding School. During the eighteenth and nineteenth centuries, the Spanish Riding School hosted many lavish masked balls and performances of knightly horsemanship that delighted Viennese nobility.

Left: **Although Lipizzaners are usually white, Lipizzaner foals are born dark and become lighter as they grow. Most Lipizzaners are fully white by the time they are ten years old, and they live for between twenty-eight and thirty-two years. Lipizzaners are trained from the time they are very young, and extremely close bonds develop between a horse and its rider over years of training.**

A Superior Breed

Lipizzaner stallions, known more casually as Lipizzaners, are admired for their ideal combination of form, grace, and docility. Like Arabian race horses, Lipizzaners are bred with the utmost care so that later generations will be similarly superior in beauty and prowess. In fact, all the Lipizzaner stallions in the Spanish Riding School and the stud farm in Piber today descend from one of six stallions — Pluto, Conversano, Favory, Neapolitano, Siglavy, and Maestoso — that were alive in the eighteenth and early nineteenth centuries.

Performances put on by the Spanish Riding School have enthralled audiences with marvelous stunts. Riders perform the capriole, in which the horse jumps upward but not forward, kicks its hind legs in midair, and then lands on the same spot. The *courbette* (kur-BET) is a spectacular move in which the horse balances on its hind legs and moves forward in hopping motions, its front legs never touching the ground. In a performance that involves several horses, choreographed steps are executed with mechanical precision and in unison. The result is an incredible sight, as if the horses were capable of ballet.

Trachten

Timeless Traditional Clothes

Before the twentieth century, *Trachten* referred to the style of coded clothing worn in German-speaking societies. People indicated whether they were from one region or another; of a higher or lower social class; married or single; or members of a particular religious group through the pieces of clothing and accessories that they wore. Today, the term "Trachten" refers to any style of rustic, traditional clothing that is regarded as timeless in its fashion appeal. Austrians today wear Trachten as an expression of national identity and pride.

Trachten For Women

In Austria, the traditional outfit for women is called the *Dirndl* (DEERN-dl). The Dirndl was inspired by Trachten for men and consists of a blouse called the *Leibl* (LEYE-bl); a long, wide skirt that may be pleated or gathered; and an often colorful apron. Some women wear a sleeveless, snug-fitting bodice over their Leibl. Other accessories include chokers, decorative bibs, and

THE ORIGIN OF THE DIRNDL

The Dirndl was originally a dress that female servants wore when they worked. *Dirn* (DEERN) means "maid," and *Dirndlgewand* (DEERN-dl-ger-VAHND) means the "maid's dress." Dialects spoken in some parts of Austria use the word *Dirndl* to mean "a young woman." Consequently, it is possible to say that a Dirndl is wearing a Dirndl.

Left: Austrians today do not observe the codes assigned in the past to the fabrics from which their traditional clothes are made, the colors of the fabric, and the styles in which the fabrics are cut and sewn together. Instead, colors and materials are chosen based on contemporary influences and trends. Trachten can be made from linen, cotton, wool, or silk.

petticoats. Women customarily wear white stockings and black leather slip-on shoes with straps that extend horizontally across the feet and fasten near the ankles when they wear the Dirndl. Elaborate ornamentation — in the form of embroidery, added lace, or frills — on various parts of the Dirndl, from the front of the skirt to the seams to the sleeves of the blouse, is common.

For Men

Men's Trachten experienced their first revival in the late 1800s, when it became fashionable for men to wear *Lederhosen* (LAY-duh-HOH-zun). Lederhosen are a pair of leather shorts that end just above the knees and are held up by suspenders. Trachten for men basically consist of a white shirt; a tie in the form of an ascot; a vest or thick, button-down woolen sweater; and Lederhosen or breeches. Breeches sometimes come with a matching formal jacket to form a fine suit. Men wearing Trachten tend to wear long socks that end just under the knees and black leather shoes that are laced up on the sides rather than the tops. Men also sometimes wear hats that are decorated with feathers or pins.

SHOWCASING TRACHTEN

The Austrian Folklore Museum, in Vienna; the Styrian Folklore Museum, in Graz; and the Tyrolean Museum of Folk Art, in Innsbruck, each contain an extensive collection of Trachten. The collections show the styles of Trachten that were popular during different periods in Austria's history.

The Trapp Family

Together with their ten children, Maria and Georg von Trapp formed a singing ensemble called the Trapp Family Singers. Their remarkable story has been immortalized in the Hollywood film *The Sound of Music* (1965).

Inspiring the Sound of Music

Maria Augusta Kutschera (1905–1987) endured a difficult childhood. In 1926, she took a job at the home of Baron Georg von Trapp, a retired naval captain, who hired her to care for his sickly daughter. Maria and Georg married in 1927. In 1938, the Nazi Germans, led by Adolf Hitler, entered Austria, and the Trapp family's privileged lifestyle came to an abrupt end. Not wanting to arouse the suspicion of the Nazi authorities, the Trapp family gave the impression that they were going on an ordinary hiking trip up the mountains. In reality, the family crossed the Austrian Alps on foot and escaped into Italian territory with little more than the clothes they were wearing. In order to make a living, the family did what they did best together — sing.

Left: **As a governess, Maria Kutschera (*middle left*) cared for the seven children of Baron Georg von Trapp (*middle right*). She married the baron in 1927 and had three children with him. The Austrian family eventually settled in Stowe, Vermont. Maria gave the name *Cor Unum,* which means "One Heart," to the family's new home in the United States. Georg von Trapp died in 1947. Some people consider the Trapp family to be Austria's most popular singers.**

The Trapp family first sang at weddings and birthdays, but their good reputation soon spread. They toured Europe with their act before arriving in the United States in 1939. That same year, they bought a farmhouse and the surrounding 600 acres (243 hectares) of land in Stowe, Vermont, because the area reminded them of Austria. In 1947, the Trapp family continued its singing tradition by setting up the Trapp Family Music Camp. The camp was so successful that additions were made to the farmhouse to accommodate more guests on the estate. With those additions, the Trapp Family Lodge came into being. It is still operating today.

The Book, the Musical, the Movies

Maria wrote a book called *The Story of the Trapp Family Singers* that was published in 1949. The book inspired two German films — *Die Trapp Familie* (1956) and its sequel *Die Trapp Familie in Amerika* (1958). Both wild successes, the German films attracted the attention of American producers, and the Trapp family's story was next transformed into a Broadway musical. The musical was first performed in late 1959 and went on to play another 1,442 shows and win six Tony Awards. By then, Hollywood was eager to turn the musical into a film. *The Sound of Music* opened in American movie theaters in 1965.

Vienna

A City Preserved

During its rich and colorful history, Vienna has twice served as an imperial city, first as the seat of the Holy Roman Empire (1558–1806) and later as the capital of the Austro-Hungarian empire (1806–1918). In 1918, Vienna became the capital of Austria, a republic formed at the end of World War I. The city became part of Adolf Hitler's "Greater" Germany during World War II (1938–1945), the end of which was followed by a decade of foreign occupation involving British, French, American, and Soviet forces. Austria regained independence in 1955, with the signing of the State Treaty. Since then, Vienna has remained the capital of Austria.

Despite its tumultuous history, Vienna remains western Europe's best preserved old-world city. The character of Vienna today is said to be largely unchanged from what it was before World War I broke out in Europe in 1914. In fact, some people believe that it is possible to live in Vienna today in much the

Below: **The Belvedere Palace in Vienna was designed by Johann Lucas von Hildebrandt, whose style became popular throughout the Habsburg lands in the eighteenth century.**

same way and at much the same pace as the Viennese themselves did one hundred years ago. The Viennese are proud of their enlightened *Lebenskunst* (leh-buhnz-KOONST), or "art of living."

Above: **Many Viennese buildings are decorated with the types of sculptures and statues that are common features of the baroque and rococo architectural styles.**

Mapping Vienna

In 2001, more than 1.5 million Austrians lived in the city of Vienna, which covers an area of about 160 square miles (414 square km). The larger metropolitan area of Vienna is only slightly greater in population, at nearly 1.9 million, but covers an area of some 1,491 square miles (3,862 square km).

For the purposes of local government, the city of Vienna is divided into twenty-three *Bezirke* (ber-ZEER-keh), or districts. At the very heart of the city is Innere Stadt, which is also known as district I. Innere Stadt is surrounded by the Ringstrasse, a circular road that separates the city's core from the inner suburbs (districts II–IX). Grand buildings and monuments can be seen on either side of the Ringstrasse. Another circular road, the Gürtel, separates the inner suburbs from the outer suburbs, which are also known as districts X–XX. The outer suburbs are mostly residential areas. Districts XXI–XXIII form the city's outskirts.

COFFEEHOUSES

After the city's baroque architecture, the Viennese coffeehouse is probably the next most famous feature of Vienna. A typical Viennese coffeehouse has twenty ways to serve a cup of coffee. Café Hawelka, Café Prückel, Café Mozart, and Demel are some of Vienna's classic coffeehouses.

Wine Taverns

A Wine-drinking Culture

Many Austrian adults are passionate about fine wines. Generations of Austrians have learned to appreciate the art of winemaking and have developed refined tastes at the country's many Heurigen. These wine taverns are run by winemakers who serve only their own creations. Many Heurigen are located in private vineyards in the Austrian countryside. Although the first Heurigen emerged in the late eighth century, these wine taverns were only legalized in the late 1700s. Since then, wine taverns have become important to the Austrian lifestyle and culture.

The term "Heurigen" also means "new wines." New wines are wines produced from the most recent harvest. New wines are launched every November and sold until December of the following year. It is a long-standing tradition among Austrians to visit Heurigen to sample new wines.

Inside a Heuriger

A typical *Heuriger* (HOY-rih-EHR) is simply furnished and unpretentious. Patrons tend to sit on wooden benches placed on either side of large wooden tables and order their choice of wines

Above: **Wine and wine taverns (*image above*) are important parts of Austrian culture. Wine production is regulated by law in the country. The different types of wine, what they should taste like, and how much of each type can be produced in a year are some of the more important issues addressed by the country's laws.**

from their seats. A Heuriger also offers its patrons a buffet of breads, cold cuts, roasted or smoked meats, sausages, cheeses, and pickles to eat while they sip their glasses of wine. Like the wines served, the various dishes are prepared on the premises and served with pride. *Heurigenplatte* (HOY-rih-GEHN PLAH-teh) is a platter of cold cuts, sausages, cheese, chopped onions, pickles, and bread.

Different Flavors from Different Regions

Vienna, Lower Austria, Styria, and Burgenland produce about 99 percent of the country's wine. Lower Austria is the country's top wine-producing region. Some regions, such as Weinviertel, have wine-producing histories that date back to the Middle Ages. Gumpoldskirchen, a white wine originating from Lower Austria,

enjoys a good reputation around the world and is arguably Austria's most famous wine export. Both southern Styria and Burgenland have warmer climates and tend to produce strong tasting wines. Burgenland is famous for the red wines called Zweigelt and Blaufränkisch, as well as quality dessert wines. Winemakers from Styria are proud of their Schilcher, which is a tart, peach-colored wine that is unique to the region. The grapes used to make Schilcher have been cultivated in Styria for centuries. Chardonnay and Traminer are flavorful white wines that are produced in Styria.

RELATIONS WITH NORTH AMERICA

In the twentieth century, North America — and especially the United States — was very important to the economic and political fate of Austria. Austria was helped through its postwar economic troubles with grants given by the United States under the Marshall Plan. Austria used those grants to rebuild its economy. Today, Austria is one of the wealthiest and most stable countries in the world. In 1955, Austria declared itself to be a neutral country. As a neutral nation, Austria played a vital role during the Cold War (1947–1991). Vienna was the venue of talks between the United States and the Soviet Union.

Opposite: **In 2003, Austrian-born American Arnold Schwarzenegger was elected governor of California. Schwarzenegger, who first gained fame as an athlete and movie star, became the thirty-eighth governor of the state of California.**

Austria and North America have maintained close political and social ties. In the nineteenth and twentieth centuries, the United States and Canada accepted Austrian immigrants and asylum seekers. Austrians, in turn, have made an impact in their new home countries. For example, Austrian-born Arnold Schwarzenegger, is a famous Hollywood actor who has recently entered U.S. politics. Austrian Frank Stronach is a successful businessman and the founder of Canada's Magna International, one of the world's largest suppliers of components and systems to the automotive industry.

Above: **In the United States, American and Austrian organizations cohost cultural and fund-raising events. The Viennese Opera Ball, sponsored by the Austrian-American Alliance for Children, is held in Washington, D.C., each year, and follows the style of Vienna's Opera Ball.**

Left: In 1948, aid in the form of food, such as flour, sugar, and eggs, was sent to Europe under the Marshall Plan. Austria received U.S. $131 per capita from the program. On a per capita basis, Austria received more aid than many of the other countries helped under the Marshall Plan.

Reconstructing Post-World War II Austria

In 1946 and 1947, Europe was in economic turmoil as a result of both the aftermath of World War II (1939–1945) and one of the harshest European winters in decades. Basic necessities, such as food, water, and shelter, were in short supply, and unemployment was high. In 1947, U.S. secretary of state George C. Marshall proposed a plan to provide humanitarian aid to war-torn Europe. This plan, formally called the European Recovery Program, later came to be known as the Marshall Plan. Under the Marshall Plan, the United States pledged to provide U.S. $13.3 billion in economic aid. This amount would be equivalent to about U.S. $100 billion in the early twenty-first century.

Austria was one of sixteen western European countries that received aid under the Marshall Plan. Between 1948 and 1953, Austria received U.S. $962 million in the form of grants and loans, food, machinery, and raw materials. Austria used the grants and loans to reconstruct its industrial sector. It built infrastructure, such as power plants, to get the Austrian economy on its feet again. Some of the money also went to building ski lifts and cable cars in order to make Alpine regions accessible to skiers and thereby jump-start Austria's tourism industry.

GEORGE C. MARSHALL (1880–1959)

George Catlett Marshall was the U.S. Army chief of staff during World War II. In 1947, he became the secretary of state. On June 5 of that year, he presented the Marshall Plan during a speech at Harvard University. Marshall was awarded the Nobel Peace Prize in 1953.

The Marshall Plan served as a milestone for U.S.-Austrian relations. In 2000, the Marshall Plan Foundation was formed in commemoration of the success of the Marshall Plan in the reconstruction of the Austrian economy. The foundation aims to strengthen Austro-American relations.

Shades of Neutrality

After the State Treaty was signed in 1955, Austria declared itself a neutral country. Since then, Austria's neutrality has aided the country in becoming a mediator in international affairs. During the years of the Cold War, Austria served as a bridge between the Soviet Union and the United States, as well as between communist and democratic Europe. Austria's capital, Vienna, became a place for the exchange of ideas and a venue for important international meetings. For example, the second round of the Strategic Arms Limitation Talks (SALT II) took place in Vienna in the 1970s.

Austria, however, has had to constantly redefine what it means to be a neutral country. Austrian leaders agree that political neutrality is different from moral neutrality. Therefore, Austria opposed the Soviet invasions of Hungary (1956) and Czechoslovakia (1968). Since the end of the Cold War in 1991 and the events following the 2001 terrorist attacks in the United States, Austria has had to reassess its role in international politics and redefine the extent of its neutrality.

Left: Delegates attend a UN meeting. Vienna is one of the permanent seats of the United Nations, and it has frequently been chosen as a venue for international diplomatic meetings.

The Waldheim Affair

The good relationship between Austria and the United States was strained in 1986 when Kurt Waldheim, the former secretary-general to the UN, was elected president of Austria. The controversy concerned Waldheim's alleged role as an intelligence officer in the German army during World War II. Waldheim was implicated in Nazi war crimes, such as the deportation of Jews to Nazi concentration camps. As a result of these alleged crimes, U.S. authorities barred Waldheim from entering the United States. Waldheim has since been cleared of the allegation that he committed war crimes.

Above: **Kurt Waldheim is the former Austrian president who was cleared of the charge that he committed wartime atrocities.**

Current Relations

Austria shares many similar policies and common interests on global issues with both the United States and Canada. Austria and Canada share similar voting patterns in the UN and are in agreement on issues such as human rights. In 2000, relations between Austria and North America, however, once again were strained in connection with Austria's Nazi past. The United States restricted contact with Austria after the right-wing Freedom Party became part of Austria's coalition government. The party's leader, Joerg Haider, had praised Naziism in the past.

AUSTRIAN-AMERICAN DAY

In 1997, U.S. president Bill Clinton declared September 26 to be Austrian-American Day. The declaration was made to commemorate the day in 1945 when officials from Austria's nine states formed a postwar provisional government in Vienna. Austrian-American Day is celebrated quietly by the country's Austrian-American community.

Left: **In November 2001, Austrian chancellor Wolfgang Schuessel (*right*) met with U.S. president George W. Bush in the Oval Office at the White House to affirm that Austria backs the war on terrorism.**

Left: **Austrian president Thomas Klestil** *(left)* **welcomes Canadian prime minister Jean Chretien** *(right)* **to Vienna during Chretien's two-day visit to Austria in 1999.**

Diplomatic relations returned to normal after nine months, when Austrian chancellor Wolfgang Schuessel announced that his administration would seek compensation for those who were forced into slavery by the Nazis.

During the 2003 war in Iraq, Austria provided humanitarian assistance for war victims. In May 2003, Austria flew eleven injured Iraqi children to Austria to be treated for their injuries, making Austria the first country to fly war victims out of Iraq. Austria is also part of the Network of Human Security, which is planning to set up a center in southern Iraq for children traumatized by war.

Economic Ties

The North American market accounts for about 4.4 percent of Austria's foreign trade. The United States is Austria's third most important trading partner in exports and imports. Austria is an important supplier of motor vehicle parts to U.S. car makers. More than four hundred U.S. businesses, which are mainly located in Vienna, operate in Austria.

The amount of trade between Austria and Canada is less than the amount of trade between Austria and the United States. Canada, however, is still an important trading partner to Austria. Canadian investments in Austria are more than twice as large as the Austrian investments in Canada.

The Early Immigrants

The first recorded Austrian immigrants came to Canada in the seventeenth century as soldiers. These early immigrants identified themselves not as Austrians but as Germans from the Habsburg Empire. In 1731, a group of Protestants from Salzburg were expelled and emigrated to the United States, forming a settlement at Ebenezer, Georgia. Many subsequent immigrants from the Habsburg lands settled in Pennsylvania, and the German-speaking population in the states of Pennsylvania, North Carolina, and Georgia grew rapidly. Some Austrian immigrants settled in urban areas, while others worked as farmers and artisans, forming small communities in the midwestern United States. Other immigrants settled in the Canadian prairies in the provinces of Alberta and Saskatchewan.

During the nineteenth and early-twentieth centuries, a wave of immigrants from the Austro-Hungarian empire arrived in Canada and the United States. These immigrants were not just Austrians but also Czechs, Croats, Slovaks, and Germans, who left their home countries because of the growing political and economic instability of the empire. Between 1926 and 1938, a large number of Austrians from Carinthia, Styria, and Burgenland settled in Canada.

Below: **Some Austrian immigrants settled in the prairies of Canada and established farms.**

Seeking Refuge

After Germany's occupation of Austria in 1938, large numbers of political refugees fled Austria, seeking refuge and political asylum in North America. Many of these political refugees were Jews who either were expelled from their home country during the Anschluss or had fled to escape Nazi persecution. The Nazis prohibited Austrian Jews from studying or working as professionals. Austrian Jews had their property seized and some were moved out of their homes and forced by the Nazis to live in ghettoes. They were constantly under threat of imprisonment and execution, leading them to go into hiding or to flee Austria to escape Nazi oppression. Between March 1938 and November 1939, more than 126,000 Jews emigrated from Austria. About 30,000 fled to the United States. Many of these refugees were academics and professionals. The number of emigrants from Austria continued to increase after World War II because of the unstable living conditions in postwar Austria. About 23,500 Viennese Jews emigrated during World War II.

North Americans of Austrian Descent

The present-day populations in the United States and Canada reflect the long history of Austrian immigration to North America. According to a 1996 census, Canada has about 140,000 Canadians of Austrian descent. They mainly live in Ontario, British Columbia, and Alberta, although some Austrian-Canadians still live on the prairies. The cities of Toronto, Montreal, and Vancouver, also have significant populations of Austrian-Canadians.

In the United States, there are more than 700,000 Americans of Austrian descent. Austrian-American communities are found in every state. The state of New York has the largest number of Austrian-Americans, followed by the states of California, Pennsylvania, Florida, and New Jersey.

Austrian Influence in North America

Many Austrians and North Americans of Austrian ancestry have made an impact on North American culture and history through their contributions in fields such as science, music, film, manufacturing, and industry. Classical guitarist Norbert Kraft,

Left: Austrian-born celebrity chef **Wolfgang Puck** (*center*) eats pizza with children at a 2001 fund-raising event in Westlake, California. California has almost 85,000 Americans of Austrian descent.

Left: **Raimund Abraham** *(right)*, **the architect of the Austrian Cultural Forum building, in New York City, speaks with the organization's director. The Austrian Cultural Forum is a leading center for the promotion of contemporary Austrian arts. Organizations such as the Austrian Cultural Forum are social centers for Austrian-Americans and expatriate Austrians living in the United States to get together and celebrate their heritage. Today, there are more than 10,000 expatriate Austrians living in the United States and about 1,200 in Canada.**

harpsichordist Greta Kraus, and composer Anton Emil Kuerti are well known in North America. Viennese scientist Hermann F. Mark developed nylon, Dacron, Orlon, and polystyrene in the United States. Austrians have also made contributions to architecture in North America. Contemporary architect Rudolf M. Schindler (1887–1953) designed a modern house that is well-suited to the California climate. His house design became a prototype for other such houses in California. Another Austrian-born American architect, Richard J. Neutra (1892–1970), is credited for designing houses in the International style.

Special clubs cater to the North American Austrian communities. Larger organizations, such as the American Austrian Foundation, in New York City; the Austrian Cultural Forum, in Washington, D.C.; and the MAK Center for Art and Architecture, in Los Angeles, represent Austria's extraordinary cultural presence in the United States. They serve as forums and meeting places for Austrians and provide information to those who are interested in Austrian culture.

Austrians in Hollywood

Some Austrians have made great impacts in Hollywood. The history of Austrians in American film began in the early twentieth century with Austrian-born U.S. film directors such as Erich von Stroheim (1885–1957), Fritz Lang (1890–1976), and Otto Preminger (1906–1986). Composers, such as Erich Wolfgang Korngold (1897–1957) and Max Steiner ((1888–1971) wrote the scores for hundreds of Hollywood films. Steiner composed the music for the film *Gone with the Wind* in 1938. One of the early stars of Hollywood was Fred Austerlitz (1899–1987), better known as Fred Astaire. Astaire's father was an Austrian immigrant. Another Austrian success in Hollywood is highly-acclaimed director and producer Billy Wilder (1906–2002). Wilder immigrated to the United States from Vienna to escape the Nazi regime. During his film career, he won six Oscars and received twenty Academy Award nominations. He received a lifetime achievement award in 1986.

Austrian actors, such as Klaus-Maria Brandauer and Helmut Qualtinger, have played several roles in American films. Arnold Schwarzenegger, however, is the most famous Austrian in Hollywood. Schwarzenegger was born in 1947 in a small town near the city of Graz, Austria. He moved to the United States in 1968, at the age of twenty-one. Schwarzenegger's acting career

Left: **Austrian-born director Billy Wilder (center) poses with American actors Jack Lemmon (left) and Walter Matthau (right) on the set of *Buddy Buddy* (1982).**

Left: Arnold Schwarzenegger is known to international audiences for his role in the *Terminator* movies. He became a U.S citizen in 1984.

began in 1970, but his breakthrough to international fame came in 1984 with his role in *The Terminator*. In 2003, Schwarzenegger became the thirty-eighth governor of the state of California. He is married to broadcast journalist Maria Shriver, who is a member of the Kennedy family.

Americans in Austria

About 14,000 U.S. citizens live in Vienna. Numerous societies and organizations, such as the Austro-American Society and the American Women's Association, provide a community for U.S. expatriates to meet and celebrate holidays together. Austrian universities have study programs and student exchanges with U.S. universities. One example of the numerous educational exchange programs available with Austria is the Fulbright Program. Since 1951, over 3,000 Austrians and 2,000 Americans have participated in the program. In 1963, the governments of the United States and Austria began funding the program. Grants are awarded to Austrian and American students, as well as to American scholars visiting Austrian universities.

MARK TWAIN IN AUSTRIA

The American author Samuel Clemens (1835–1910), better known as Mark Twain, and his family lived in Vienna from 1897 to 1899. During their stay in Vienna, Twain wrote several essays, such as *Stirring Times in Austria*, which was about the events occurring in the Austro-Hungarian empire. In 1992, Twain's life and his literary works from his Austrian experience were published in a book entitled *Our Famous Guest: Mark Twain in Vienna*. The book is based on the diaries and letters penned by Twain during his stay in Austria.

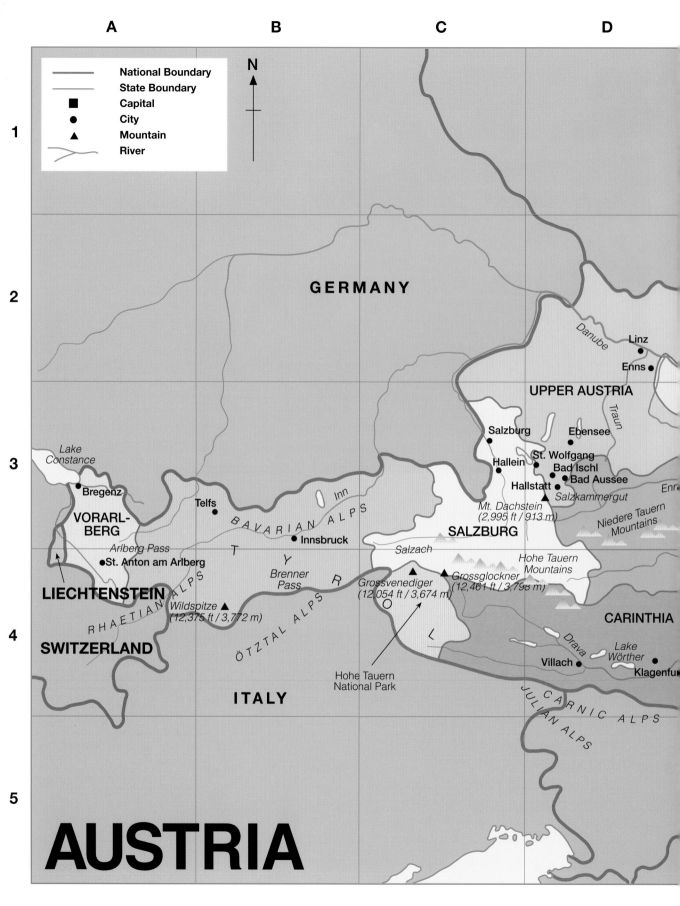

Map Legend

——	National Boundary
——	State Boundary
■	Capital
●	City
▲	Mountain
∿	River

N

GERMANY

Danube

Linz
Enns

UPPER AUSTRIA

Traun

Lake Constance

Bregenz

VORARL-BERG

Salzburg

Ebensee

St. Wolfgang

Hallein

Bad Ischl

Bad Aussee

Hallstatt

Salzkammergut

Enn

Telfs

BAVARIAN ALPS

Inn

Mt. Dachstein
(2,995 ft / 913 m)

Niedere Tauern Mountains

Arlberg Pass

Innsbruck

SALZBURG

St. Anton am Arlberg

Salzach

Hohe Tauern Mountains

T

Y

Brenner Pass

R

Grossvenediger
(12,054 ft / 3,674 m)

Grossglockner
(12,461 ft / 3,798 m)

LIECHTENSTEIN

RHAETIAN ALPS

Wildspitze
(12,375 ft / 3,772 m)

Ö T Z T A L   A L P S

O

CARINTHIA

L

Drava

Lake Wörther

SWITZERLAND

Villach

Klagenfu

Hohe Tauern National Park

ITALY

JULIAN ALPS

C A R N I C   A L P S

AUSTRIA

E **F**

CZECH REPUBLIC

LOWER AUSTRIA

Krems   Dürnstein

Wachau Valley

Melk   V a l l e y

VIENNA

D a n u b e

SLOVAKIA

Leitha

Neusiedler Lake

Eisenstadt

Semmering Pass

Mürz

STYRIA

Mur

Piber   Graz

National Park
Neusiedlersee
(Seewinkle)

Rabnitz

BURGENLAND

HUNGARY

SLOVENIA

CROATIA

Arlberg Pass A4

Bad Aussee D3
Bad Ischl D3
Bavarian Alps B3–C3
Bregenz A3
Brenner Pass B4
Burgenland F2–F4

Carinthia C4–F4
Carnic Alps D4–D5
Croatia E5–F5
Czech Republic C1–F2

Dachstein, Mt. D3
Danube (Donau) River
    A2–F2
Danube Valley D2–E2
Drava (Drau) River
    C4–F5
Dürnstein E2

Ebensee D3
Eisenstadt F3
Enns D2
Enns River D2–D3

Germany A1–C3
Graz E4
Grossglockner C4
Grossvenediger C4

Hallein C3
Hallstatt D3
Hohe Tauern Mountains
    C3–D4
Hohe Tauern National
    Park C4
Hungary F3–F5

Inn River A4–D2
Innsbruck B3
Italy A4–D5

Julian Alps C4–D5

Klagenfurt D4
Krems E2

Lake Constance
    (Bodensee) A3

Lake Wörther D4
Leitha River E3–F3
Liechtenstein A3–A4
Linz D2
Lower Austria E2–F3

Melk E2
Mur (Mura) River D4–E3
Mürz River E3

National Park
    Neusiedlersee
    (Seewinkle) F3
Neuseidler Lake F3

Ötztal Alps B4

Piber E4

Rabnitz River F3
Rhaetian Alps A4

Salzach River C2–C3
Salzburg (city) C3
Salzburg (state) C3–D4
Salzkammergut D3
Semmering Pass E3
Slovakia F2–F3
Slovenia D4–F4
St. Anton am Arlberg
    A4
St. Wolfgang D3
Styria D3–E4
Switzerland A3–A5

Tauern Mountains
    C4–D3
Telfs B3
Traun River D2–D3
Tyrol A3–C4

Upper Austria C2–E2

Vienna (city) F2
Vienna (state) F2
Villach D4
Vorarlberg A3–A4

Wachau Valley E2
Wildspitze B4

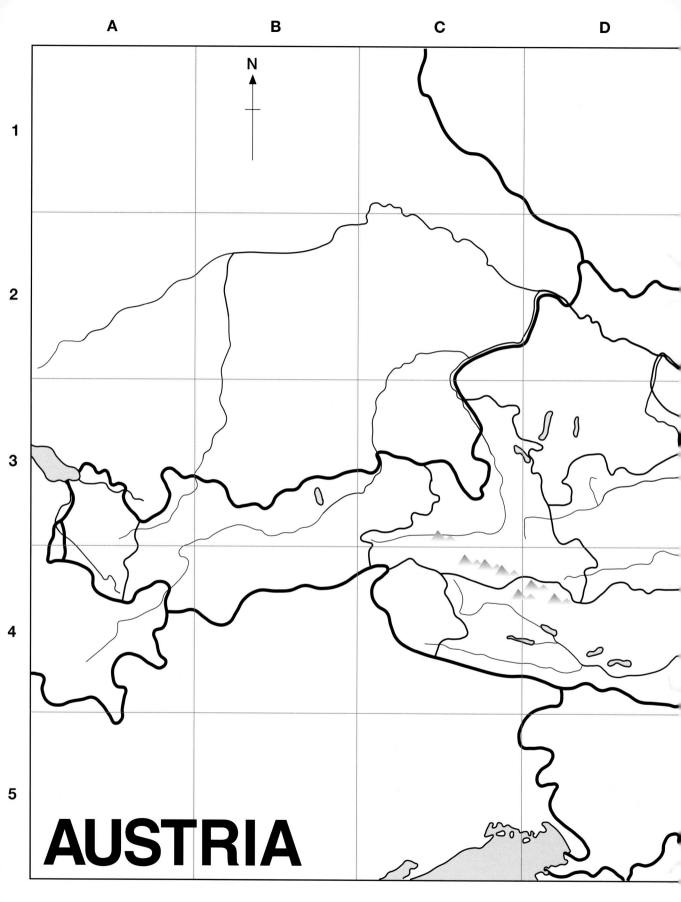

A   B   C   D

N

1

2

3

4

5

AUSTRIA

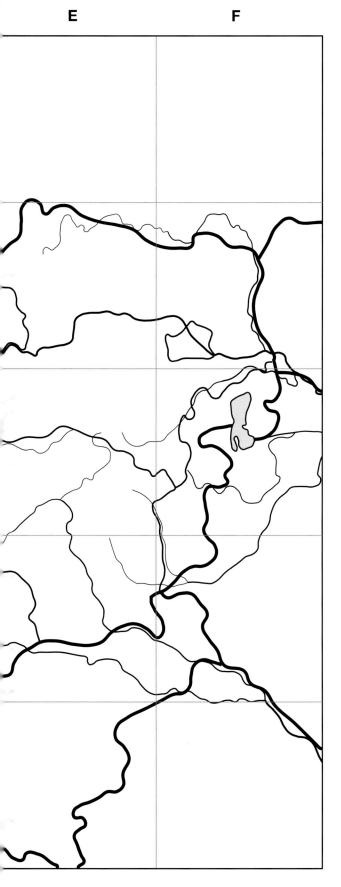

E   F

How Is Your Geography?

Learning to identify the main geographical areas and points of a country can be challenging. Although it may seem difficult at first to memorize the locations and spellings of major cities or the names of mountain ranges, rivers, deserts, lakes, and other prominent physical features, the end result of this effort can be very rewarding. Places you previously did not know existed will suddenly come to life when referred to in world news, whether in newspapers, television reports, other books and reference sources, or on the Internet. This knowledge will make you feel a bit closer to the rest of the world, with its fascinating variety of cultures and physical geography.

This map can be duplicated for use in a classroom. (PLEASE DO NOT WRITE IN THIS BOOK!) Students can then fill in any requested information on their individual map copies. The student can also make a copy of the map and use it as a study tool to practice identifying place names and geographical features on his or her own.

Austria at a Glance

Official Name   Republic of Austria (Republik Österreich)

Capital   Vienna (Wien)

Official Language   German

Population   8,188,207 (July 2003 estimate)

Land Area   32,377 square miles (83,857 square km)

States   Burgenland, Carinthia (Kaernten), Lower Austria (Niederoesterreich),Upper Austria (Oberoesterreich), Salzburg, Styria (Steiermark), Tyrol (Tirol), Vorarlberg, Vienna (Wien)

Highest Point   Grossglockner 12,461 feet (3,798 m)

Lowest Point   Neusiedler Lake 377 feet (115 m)

Border Countries   Czech Republic, Germany, Hungary, Italy, Liechtenstein, Slovakia, Slovenia, Switzerland

Major River   Danube (Donau)

Major Lakes   Neusiedler Lake (Neusiedlersee), Lake Constance (Bodensee)

Major Cities   Graz, Innsbruck, Linz, Salzburg, Vienna

Major Religions   Roman Catholic (78 percent), Protestant (5 percent), Muslim (4 percent), other (13 percent)

National Anthem   Österreichische Bundeshymne (Austrian National Anthem)

Major Exports   machinery and equipment, motor vehicles and parts, paper and paperboard, metal goods, chemicals, iron and steel, textiles, foodstuffs

Major Imports   machinery and equipment, motor vehicles, chemicals, metal goods, oil and oil products, foodstuffs

Currency   Euro (0.828 Euro = U.S. $1 in 2004)

Opposite: **A carved tree stump located in the Salzkammergut region, a popular family vacation region.**

Glossary

German Vocabulary

Anschluss (AHN-SHLOOS): the union between Austria and Germany in 1938.

Apfelstrudel (ahp-FEHL-stroo-DEHL): a baked pastry filled with diced apples and raisins.

Bezirke (ber-ZEER-keh): districts.

Dirn (d-EERN): a maid.

Dirndl (d-EERN-dl): traditional Austrian dress for women consisting of an embroidered blouse, a lace bodice, a full skirt, and an apron.

Dirndlgewand (DEERN-dl-ger-VAHND): a maid's dress.

Fasching (fah-SHING): a celebration before Lent, marked by fancy dress parades.

Gemuetlichkeit (GEH-moot-lihk-EYET): a relaxed enjoyment of life.

Gulasch (GOO-lahsh): a spicy beef stew.

Hauptschule (HOWPT-schoo-luh): middle or secondary school.

Heurigen (HOY-rih-GEHN): wine taverns.

Heuriger (HOY-rih-EHR): a wine tavern.

Heurigenplatte (HOY-rih-GEHN-PLAH-teh): a platter of cold cuts, sausages, cheeses, onions, pickles, and breads.

Hochdeutsch (hoch-DOYTCH): a dialect of German that originated in the German highlands. Hochdeutsch is the official spoken language in Austria.

Kaffeehaus (KAH-fay-HOWSS): a coffeehouse.

Knödel (NOH-dehl): dumplings that are filled with sweet or savory fillings.

Kuemmelbraten (kuh-MEHL-brah-TEHN): hot, sliced pork with crispy skin.

Länder (LEN-der): self-governing states.

Landtag (LAHN-tahg): an Austrian state's legislative body.

Lebenskunst (leh-buhnz-KOONST): the art of living.

Lederhosen (LAY-duh-HOH-zun): knee-high leather shorts with suspenders.

Leibl (LEYE-bl): a long, wide, pleated or gathered skirt.

Lipizzaner (lee-pee-ZAH-nehr): a breed of prized white horses.

Palmkätzchen (palm-KETZ-chen): braided pussy willow branches that signify rebirth.

Reifeprüfung (REYE-feh-PROO-foong): the diploma awarded at the end of a Hauptschule education.

Sachertorte (SAH-kehr-TOHR-teh): a rich chocolate cake.

Sezession (ZEH-zee-on): an art movement that began in the 1890s and involved German and Austrian artists who broke away from academic art to form their own style of art.

Surbraten (SOOR-brah-TEHN): a cooked pickled meat that is commonly served at Heurigen.

Tafelspitz (TAH-fehl-SPEETZ): a dish of boiled beef.

Trachten (TRAHK-tun): traditional rustic Austrian outfits. Singular is *Tracht*.

Vanillekipferl (van-ill-leh-KIP-fuhrl): vanilla cookies that are usually eaten at Christmas.

Volksschule (FOLK-schoo-luh): a four-year elementary school.

Vorarlbergerische (for-ARL-BER-ger-ish-eh): Austrian dialect spoken in Vorarlberg.

Wiener Backhendel (VEE-nah-BAHK-hayn-dl): Viennese fried chicken.

Wienerische (VEE-ner-RISH-eh): an Austrian-Bavarian dialect spoken in Vienna.

English Vocabulary

abodes: homes or residences.

affluent: prosperous.

Allies: the group of countries, including the United States, Great Britain, and France, that joined forces in World War I against the Central Powers (Germany, Austria-Hungary, and Turkey) and, along with the Soviet Union, in World War II against the Axis (Germany, Italy, and Japan).

ascot: a tie or scarf with broad ends looped to lie flat one upon the other and sometimes held with a pin.

biodiversity: the variety of plant and animal species in an environment.

bourgeoisie: the middle class.

breeches: knee-length trousers often with decoration along the bottom edges.

commission: authorization or assignment to perform a task.

deciduous trees: trees that shed their leaves annually.

docility: the characteristic of being easily managed or readily trained.

ecotourism: tourism that respects the beauty and spectacle of an area's natural environment.

enlightened: freed of ignorance, false beliefs, or prejudice.

ensemble: a group of singers or musicians.

equestrian: relating to horseback riding.

governess: a woman whose job it is to care for and supervise one or more children in the household.

haunts: places that are frequently visited.

homogenous: consisting of the same type of parts throughout.

hydroelectricity: electricity generated by waterpower.

laureates: people who have received an honor for an accomplishment in an art or science.

mediator: one who helps to bring about an agreement between two or more disagreeing parties.

neuroses: mental and emotional disorders that are accompanied by physical or psychological symptoms.

nostalgic: in the state of feeling sentimental and longing for people, places, and things belonging to the past.

patronage: support or sponsorship.

planetarium: a device that produces a representation of the heavens by the use of moving projectors.

prowess: exceptional ability, skill, or strength.

psychoanalysis: the theory and method of treating disorders of the mind originated by Sigmund Freud.

quaint: unusual or different in a way that is pleasingly old-fashioned.

repressed: excluded from consciousness.

resplendent: splendid or dazzling.

rustic: having the characteristics of rural life.

sovereignty: freedom from external control.

More Books to Read

Austria. Cultures of the World series. Sean Sheehan (Benchmark)

Austria. Enchantment of the World series. R. Conrad Stein (Children's Press Publishing)

Austria. Modern World Nations series. Alan Allport (Chelsea House Publishers)

Maria Von Trapp: Beyond the Sound of Music. Trailblazer Biography series.
    Candice F. Ransom (Carolrhoda Books)

One Eye Laughing, the Other Weeping. Dear America series. Barry Denenberg
    (Scholastic)

Life and Times of Wolfgang Amadeus Mozart. Masters of Music series. John Bankston
    (Mitchell Lane Publishers.)

Sigmund Freud: Pioneer of the Mind. Catherine Reef (Houghton Mifflin)

The Lipizzaners: Horsemanship and the Spanish Riding School of Vienna. Philippe Dumas
    (Prentice Hall)

Vienna. Cities of the World series. R. Conrad Stein (Children's Press)

Videos

Austria–Vienna. (Education 2000)

Austria: Vienna and the Danube, Salzburg and the Lakes District. (Questar)

Austria: Journeys Through the Salt Mines (The Greatest Journeys on Earth). (Janson Media)

The Sound of Music. (Fox Home Entertainment)

Web Sites

www.austria.org/

www.essentialsofmusic.com/composer/mozart.html

www.odci.gov/cia/publications/factbook/geos/au.html

www.wien.gv.at/english/

Due to the dynamic nature of the Internet, some web sites stay current longer than others. To find additional web sites, use a reliable search engine with one or more of the following keywords to help you locate information about Austria. Keywords: *Alps, Austro-Hungarian Empire, Habsburgs, Danube, Mozart, Vienna, Vienna Boys Choir.*

Index